HÄGAR

THE HORRIBLE

Haga

by Dik Browne

ATTICA
PUBLICATIONS

Introducing . . .

HÄGAR THE HORRIBLE a hard-working Barbarian businessman. He's in sacking and looting.

His wife, HELGA. She finds civilising Hägar a 24-hour-a-day job!

This is HAMLET, their son, a real problem child! He insists on wearing his hair short, bathing, reading and otherwise behaving in a very unbarbarian manner.

HONI, their daughter, is sixteen years old, and still not married!

But that's not the end of Hagars troubles . . . there's also LUCKY EDDIE who must be the most hopeless assistant in history!

COPYRIGHT © 1986 King Features Syndicate, Inc. World rights reserved

Yaffa Character Licensing

First published by Attica Publications 1986

Attica Publications is an imprint of Attica Limited, DLM House, Edinburgh Way, Harlow, Essex CM20 2HL, England.

ISBN 1 85176 049 0

Printed and bound in Great Britain by Cox & Wyman Ltd, Reading

THANK YOU FOR NOT SMOKING

DIK BROWNE

© 1983 King Features Syndicate, Inc. World rights reserved.

MY HAGAR IS VERY ORGANISED... HE WORKS 8 HOURS...

HE SLEEPS 8 HOURS...

AND HE EATS 8 HOURS

Dik Browne

JUST RUNNING DOWN TO THE LOCAL STORE FOR SOME MORE HORRIBLY GOOD CARTOON BOOKS, COLOUR ALBUMS, CALENDARS, DIARIES, REMINDER CALENDARS, GREETING CARDS, GIFTWRAP AND TAGS – ALL FEATURING ME OF COURSE!
WHY NOT JOIN ME BEFORE THE BARBARIANS GET THERE!

Hagar Books to Collect:

POCKET BOOKS

Hagar Tries Again
Hagar Has A Go
Hagar In A Fix
Hagar On The Rampage
Hagar Gets It All
Hagar In The Rough
Hagar Leads The Way
Hagar Takes A Break
Hagar All At Sea
Hagar On Holiday

COLOUR ALBUMS

Hagar Lets Himself Go
Hagar In Trouble
Hagar The Hero

COLOUR CARTOON BOOKS

Hagar Tells It Like It Is
Hagar Never Say Die

BLACK & WHITE CARTOON BOOKS

Hagar Meets His Match
Hagar In A Hurry

Available soon...
Hagar the Horrible's Viking Handbook

Pocket Rough Guide

LAS VEGAS

written and researched by

GREG WARD

Contents

INTRODUCTION TO
LAS VEGAS

A dazzling oasis where forty million people a year let their hair down, Las Vegas has made a fine art of indulging its visitors' every appetite. From its ever-changing architecture to cascading chocolate fountains, adrenaline-pumping zip lines and jaw-dropping stage shows, everything is built to thrill; as soon as the novelty wears off, it's blown up and replaced with something bigger and better. Not only does the city hold the largest hotels in the world, but that's pretty much all it holds; it's these extraordinary creations that everyone comes to see.

Best places to get a view of the Strip

Although towering hotel blocks jostle for position along the Strip, there are surprisingly few places that offer non-guests a panoramic view of the whole thing. Possibilities include the summit of the Stratosphere (but that's a little far north and not quite aligned with the Strip), and the Voodoo Rooftop Nightclub at the Rio, off to one side. So the winner is – the observation platform at the top of Paris's Eiffel Tower (see p.57), perfectly poised to look north and south along the Strip's busiest stretch, as well as west, and down, to the fountains of Bellagio.

Each hotel is a neighbourhood in its own right, measuring as much as a mile end to end; crammed full of state-of-the-art clubs, restaurants, spas and pools; and centring on what makes the whole thing possible – an action-packed casino where tourists and tycoons alike are gripped by the roll of the dice and the turn of the card.

Even if its entire urban area covers 136 square miles, most visitors see no more of Las Vegas than two short, and very different, linear stretches. Downtown, the original centre, now amounts to four brief (roofed-over) blocks of Fremont Street, while the Strip begins a couple of miles south, just beyond the city limits, and runs for four miles southwest. It's the Strip where the real action is, a visual feast where each mega-casino vies to outdo the next with some outlandish

theme, be it an Egyptian pyramid (Luxor), a Roman extravaganza (Caesars Palace), a fairytale castle (Excalibur) or a European city (Paris and the Venetian).

In 1940, Las Vegas was home to just eight thousand people. It owes its extraordinary growth to its constant willingness to adapt; far from remaining kitsch and old-fashioned, it's forever reinventing itself. Entrepreneurs race to spot the latest shift in who has the money and what they want to spend it on. A few years ago the casinos realized that gamblers were happy to pay premium prices for good food; top chefs now run gourmet restaurants in venues like Bellagio and the Cosmopolitan. More recently, demand from younger visitors has prompted casinos like Wynn Las Vegas to open high-tech nightclubs to match those of Miami and LA.

NEW YORK–NEW YORK

The reputation Las Vegas still enjoys, of being a quasi-legal adult playground where (almost) anything goes, dates back to its early years when most of its first generation of luxury resorts were cut-throat rivals controlled by The Mob. In those days illegal profits could easily be "skimmed" off and respectable investors steered clear. Then, as now, visitors loved to imagine that they were rubbing shoulders with gangsters. Standing well back from the Strip, each casino was a labyrinth in which it was all but impossible to find an exit. During the 1980s, however, visitors started to explore on foot; mogul Steve Wynn cashed in by placing a flame-spouting volcano outside his new Mirage. As the casinos competed to lure in pedestrians, they filled in the daunting distances from the sidewalk, and between casinos.

With Las Vegas booming in the 1990s, gaming corporations bought up first individual casinos, and then each other. The Strip today is dominated by just two colossal conglomerates – MGM Resorts and Caesars Entertainment. Once you own the casino next door, there's no reason to make each a virtual prison; the Strip has therefore opened out, so that much of its central portion now consists of open-air terraces and pavilions housing bars and restaurants.

The city may have tamed its setting, but the magnificent wildernesses of the American West still lie on its doorstep. Dramatic parks like Red Rock Canyon and the Valley of Fire are just a short drive away, or you can fly to the Grand Canyon, and Utah's glorious Zion National Park makes a wonderful overnight getaway.

When to visit

Visitors flock to Las Vegas throughout the year, however the climate varies enormously. In July and August, the average daytime high exceeds 100°F (38°C), while in winter the thermometer regularly drops below freezing. Hotel swimming pools generally open between April and September only.

It's which day you visit that you should really take into account; accommodation can easily cost twice as much on Friday and Saturday as during the rest of the week.

LAS VEGAS AT A GLANCE

>> EATING

Las Vegas used to be a byword for bad food, with just the occasional mobster-dominated steakhouse or Italian restaurant to relieve the monotony of the pile-'em-high **buffets**. Those days have long gone. Every major **Strip casino** now holds half a dozen or more high-quality restaurants, many run by top chefs from all over the world. Prices have soared, to a typical minimum spend of $50 per head at big-name places, but so too have standards, and you could eat a great meal in a different restaurant every night in casinos such as **Aria**, **Bellagio**, **Caesars Palace**, the **Cosmopolitan** and the **Venetian**.

>> DRINKING

Every Las Vegas casino offers free drinks to gamblers. Sit at a slot machine or gaming table, and a cocktail waitress will find you and take your order; tips are expected. In addition, the casinos hold all kinds of bars and lounges; very few tourists venture further afield to drink. Along the Strip bars tend to be themed, as with the Irish pubs of **New York–New York** or the flamboyant lounges of **Caesars Palace**; downtown they're a bit more rough-and-ready. Note that the legal drinking age is 21 – you must carry ID to prove it.

>> NIGHTLIFE

The Strip is once more riding high as the entertainment epicentre of the world. While Elvis may have left the building, headliners like **Elton John** and **Celine Dion** attract thousands of big-spending fans night after night and all the major touring acts pass through. Meanwhile the old-style feathers-and-sequins revues have been supplanted by a never-ending stream of jaw-droppingly lavish shows by the **Cirque du Soleil**, plus the likes of the postmodern **Blue Man Group**. A new generation of visitors has been responsible for the dramatic growth in the city's clubbing scene. Casinos like the **Cosmopolitan**, the **Palms** and **Wynn Las Vegas** now boast some of the world's most spectacular – and expensive – nightclubs and ultra-lounges.

>> SHOPPING

Shopping now ranks among the principal reasons that people visit Las Vegas. **Downtown** is all but devoid of shops, however, and while the workaday city holds its fair share of suburban malls, tourists do almost all of their shopping on **the Strip** itself. Their prime destination is the amazing **Forum** at Caesars Palace, followed by the **Grand Canal Shoppes** at the Venetian and **Miracle Mile** at Planet Hollywood. There are also a couple of stand-alone malls – **Fashion Show** opposite Wynn Las Vegas, which is the most useful for everyday purchases, and the very high-end **Crystals** in CityCenter.

OUR RECOMMENDATIONS FOR WHERE TO EAT, DRINK AND SHOP ARE LISTED AT THE END OF EACH CHAPTER.

Day One in Las Vegas

1 Jean Philippe Patisserie, Bellagio
> p.51. Head to the back of Bellagio to enjoy a morning pick-me-up and pastries while admiring the world's largest chocolate fountain.

2 The Conservatory, Bellagio
> p.49. Part greenhouse, part camp and colourful fantasyland, Bellagio's indoor flower show must be seen to be believed.

3 Eiffel Tower Experience > p.57. Ride into the skies atop Las Vegas's own miniature version of Paris and look down on the rest of the Strip.

Lunch > p.64. Enjoy a quintessentially French bistro meal, with a ringside seat on the Strip, at *Mon Ami Gabi* in Paris.

4 The Forum Shops > p.62. Marble statues, fountains and a false sky that cycles hourly between day and night; is it ancient Rome or simply Caesars Palace?

5 Grand Canal Shoppes > p.77. Operatic gondoliers ply the waters of the Grand Canal, serenading shoppers perusing the Venetian's upstairs, upmarket mall.

6 V Bar, the Venetian > p.82. Start your evening with a martini or cocktail in one of the Venetian's chic, sophisticated bars.

Dinner > p.81. Pan-Asian food and lush red decor at *Wazuzu* in Wynn Las Vegas combine to offer a memorable dining experience.

7 Love, the Mirage > p.84. Las Vegas's favourite Canadian clowns, the Cirque du Soleil, join forces with the Beatles to stunning effect.

Day Two in Las Vegas

1 **Il Fornaio, New York–New York** > p.40. This New York-style Italian bakery is the perfect place to grab breakfast.

2 **The Big Apple Coaster, New York–New York** > p.36. Let's shake things up – loop around the Manhattan skyline in a little yellow cab, upside down, at 70mph.

3 **Excalibur** > p.34. If things haven't been kitsch enough yet, stroll through this bizarre Arthurian castle-casino.

4 **Luxor** > p.33. Things are getting weirder – enter an Egyptian pyramid through the paws of the Sphinx to see... artefacts recovered from the *Titanic*.

5 **Shark Reef, Mandalay Bay** > p.31. Watch crocodiles and sharks swim amid the ruins of a Mayan temple.

🍴 **Lunch** > p.39. Break for a Mexican meal beside Mandalay Bay's wave pool, at the *Border Grill*.

6 **CSI The Experience, MGM Grand** > p.37. After lunch use your razor-sharp forensic skills to solve a murder.

7 **Art collection, CityCenter** > p.47. Standing aloof from the Strip, the sleek, modernist CityCenter district holds a surprising array of contemporary sculptures from the likes of Maya Lin, Henry Moore and Antony Gormley.

8 **The Shops at Crystals** > p.50. The flamboyant interior of Las Vegas's priciest mall is well worth seeing.

🍴 **Dinner** > p.52. Dine on superb "new Italian" food in *Scarpetta*, overlooking Bellagio's fountains.

9 **Jersey Boys** > p.67. Las Vegas doesn't always get Broadway right, but this romp of a musical goes down a storm in Paris.

Classic Las Vegas

If you yearn for the days when casinos smelled of mobster menace and the Rat Pack ruled the Strip, the new, corporate-owned Las Vegas can sometimes feel too tasteful for comfort. Vestiges of the bad old days still survive, though, if you know where to look.

1 The Flamingo > p.60. Okay, so the Flamingo these days is more Donny Osmond than Bugsy Siegel, but the original Strip resort still holds plenty of classic kitsch, including its trademark pink flamingoes.

2 Caesars Palace > p.58. With its half-naked centurions and Cleopatras, Caesars is where the Strip first veered towards full-on fantasy fifty years ago – and it hasn't let up since.

Lunch > p.91. The all-you-can-eat buffet is one tradition Las Vegas will never let go; prices have risen on the Strip, but head downtown and you'll find amazing value, at the *Paradise Buffet* for example.

3 The Mob Museum > p.90. There's no better place to learn the seedy story of Las Vegas's shady past than at this gripping, gruesome museum downtown.

4 El Cortez > p.89. For the true Las Vegas experience, gamble in downtown's least-changed casino, with its hard-bitten characters and rock-bottom odds.

5 Fremont Street Experience > p.86. All bright lights and flashing neon, downtown's must-see block-spanning canopy is pure old-fashioned spectacle.

Dinner > p.92. Former mayor Oscar Goodman's steakhouse, *Oscar's Beef * Booze * Broads*, oozes unabashed love for downtown's long-lost heyday.

6 Jubilee! > p.67. With its cheesy sets and high-kicking showgirls, the city's last surviving tits'n'tassles revue, at Bally's on the Strip, is a hugely enjoyable throwback.

Budget Las Vegas

While Las Vegas is not the budget destination it used to be, it's still possible to visit on the cheap if you play your cards right (better still, don't play cards at all...).

1 Excalibur > p.116. Wake up in your "wide-screen" room at Excalibur – from $50 for a large suite, they're the Strip's best value.

2 Free monorails > p.126. Hop on the free monorail system to see Luxor and Mandalay Bay.

3 The Deuce > p.125. Ride the Deuce bus north from Mandalay Bay and enjoy the Strip in all its glory.

4 The Midway > p.75. Stop off at Circus Circus to watch free circus performances on the Midway stage.

Lunch > p.62. Head for Caesars Palace and buy a "Buffet of Buffets" pass, valid for 24 hours at all Caesars' properties. Start with the *Bacchanal Buffet*, which epitomizes decadent Las Vegas excess.

5 Mac King > p.67. Cross the Strip to Harrah's to enjoy the best-value show in town – the clownish, endearing Mac King and his family-fun comedy magic.

6 Big Elvis > p.66. Simply stay in Harrah's and head for the no-cover Piano Bar, where the hunka-hunka love that is Pete Vallee keeps on burning all afternoon.

7 The Volcano > p.69. Once darkness falls, take your place outside the Mirage and watch the volcano erupt.

Dinner > p.62. Use your "Buffet of Buffets" pass again to sample the irresistible selection of all-French cuisine at *Le Village Buffet* in Paris.

8 Bellagio Fountains > p.49. The mesmerizing jets of this free water ballet make a suitably soothing end to the day.

11

Big sights

1 **The Venetian** Festooned with dazzling frescoes and echoing to the song of costumed gondoliers, the opulent Venetian is loved by kids, clubbers and culture vultures alike. > **p.71**

2 Bellagio Las Vegas at its most luxurious, an Italianate marble extravaganza with its own eight-acre lake. > **p.48**

4 Hoover Dam A mighty wall of concrete holding back the Colorado River – the architectural showpiece that made Las Vegas possible. > **p.106**

3 Fremont Street Experience Where else has the sheer chutzpah to roof over four entire city blocks just so they can project multicoloured snakes and aliens onto the ceiling? > **p.86**

5 Caesars Palace This huge and ever-playful casino is a city in itself – and an ancient Roman one at that. > **p.58**

15

Shows

1 Kà For sheer spectacle and breathtaking stunts, the most jaw-dropping Cirque show in town. **> p.43**

2 Terry Fator
Old-fashioned family entertainment, taken to another dimension thanks to ventriloquist Fator's uncanny singing skills. > **p.85**

3 Blue Man Group A bizarre but compelling blend of performance art, slapstick and high-octane rock. > **p.53**

4 Love Cirque meets the Beatles, in a double whammy of music and performance. > **p.84**

5 Jubilee! The last of the great chorus-line, ostrich-feather Las Vegas revues – catch it while you can. > **p.67**

Restaurants

1 Bouchon, the Venetian The menu at Thomas Keller's French bistro is every bit as special as the setting, on an elegant upper-storey patio. > **p.78**

2 Mon Ami Gabi, Paris The perfect venue for an al fresco French lunch, on a sidewalk patio beneath Paris's Eiffel Tower. > **p.64**

3 Beijing Noodle no. 9, Caesars Dazzling futuristic decor makes this mid-priced pan-Asian diner a truly memorable experience. > **p.63**

4 Scarpetta, Cosmopolitan Watch the Bellagio fountains as you savour Scott Conant's wonderful contemporary take on Italian cuisine. > **p.52**

5 Jean Philippe Patisserie, Bellagio Pastries and drinks to die for, given an extra air of indulgence by the extraordinary, swirling chocolate fountain. > **p.51**

Offbeat exhibits

1 Titanic: The Artifact Exhibition The world's only permanent display of *Titanic* artefacts, including a huge and very eerie chunk of the ship herself, upstairs in the Luxor pyramid. ▶ **p.33**

2 The Mob Museum
Downtown's prestigious new museum tells the story of the men who made Las Vegas – and the men who arrested them. > **p.90**

3 Secret Garden and Dolphin Habitat Siegfried and Roy are long gone from the Mirage, but their famed white tigers (and lions) are still prowling the gardens. > **p.69**

4 Bodies...the Exhibition What better place to look for dead bodies than a gigantic pyramid? Luxor makes an obvious home for this gruesome but uplifting exhibit. > **p.34**

5 CSI: The Experience A hugely enjoyable interactive adventure, in which visitors can try their wits to solve a mysterious recent murder. > **p.37**

Shopping

1 **Miracle Mile Shops** With larger stores, and more of them, the best Strip mall for leisurely browsing and shopping around. **> p.62**

2 Grand Canal Shoppes As much for souvenir hunters and sightseers as serious shoppers, the Venetian's Grand Canal is a great place for window-shopping. **> p.77**

4 The Forum Shops America's most profitable shopping mall, stuffed inside the faux Roman pomp of Caesars Palace – though the price tags are real enough. **> p.62**

3 Fashion Show The one Strip mall not linked to a casino offers large department stores as well as designer boutiques, across from Wynn Las Vegas. **> p.77**

5 Town Square At the far southern end of the Strip, this locals' favourite is not so much a mall as an outdoor shopping neighbourhood. **> p.38**

Thrill rides

1 The Big Apple Coaster Climb aboard a tiny yellow taxi-cab and loop the loop around New York–New York. > **p.36**

2 Dig This! If you've always wanted to drive a bulldozer, or play basketball with a giant digger, this is where your dreams come true. > **p.94**

4 Stratosphere Thrill Rides The craziest thrill rides of all – spin off the Stratosphere strapped to a lurching bench or simply jump off the edge. > **p.76**

3 SlotZilla Zip lines are the new big thing in Las Vegas; this one lets you slide the length of the Fremont Street Experience. > **p.87**

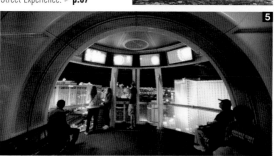

5 Las Vegas High Roller The world's biggest observation wheel, 550ft high, commands tremendous views over the city. > **p.61**

25

The deserts

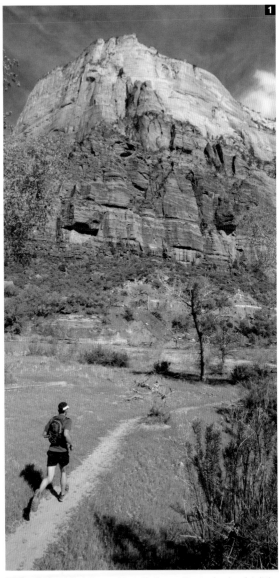

1 **Zion National Park** You can drive to Utah's magnificent red-rock park in little more than two hours to enjoy dramatic scenery and breathtaking hikes. > **p.110**

2 Valley of Fire Lurid desert scenery, bizarre rock formations and supremely remote hiking. > **p.107**

3 Grand Canyon South Rim Seeing Arizona's world-famous wonder makes a fabulous weekend road trip, but you can also fly there and back in a day. > **p.109**

4 Red Rock Canyon Las Vegas's great escape; hike and bike amid stunning red-rock sandscapes just twenty miles from the Strip. > **p.104**

5 Grand Canyon West Venture out onto the Skywalk or take a helicopter ride down to the Colorado River; the West Rim is a pricey day-trip by air, but you won't forget the adventure. > **p.108**

PLACES

The South Strip

For seven decades huge casinos have pushed ever further south along Las Vegas Boulevard, and what constitutes the South Strip has been repeatedly redefined. One thing has remained constant, however: entrepreneurs love to build lavish, eye-catching properties here because they're the first to be seen by drivers arriving from southern California. The current generation thus includes a scale model of Manhattan, New York–New York; the vast MGM Grand; a fantasy castle, Excalibur; an Egyptian pyramid, Luxor; and what's currently the true start of the Strip, the gleaming tropical paradise of Mandalay Bay. Thanks to successive buyouts and mergers, all these five are now owned by MGM Resorts and run as a cohesive unit. The exception, the ageing Tropicana, has not surprisingly struggled to keep up.

MANDALAY BAY

3950 Las Vegas Blvd S ☎ 702 632 7777, ⓦ mandalaybay.com. MAP P.32, POCKET MAP B7

The southernmost mega-casino on the Strip, **Mandalay Bay**, consists of two golden skyscrapers that tower over a sprawling complex covering a greater area than any other single property in Las Vegas. Linked to Luxor (see p.33) and Excalibur (p.34) by a stand-alone outdoor **monorail** as well as indoor walkways, it belongs to the same owners, MGM Resorts. It was built in 1999 to provide a more sophisticated alternative to what were then its more overtly child-oriented neighbours, and apart from the **Shark Reef** aquarium (see p.31) offers little to lure in casual sightseers.

Beyond a certain vague

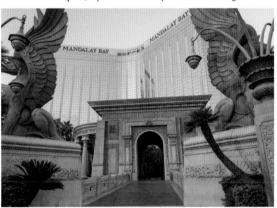

"Welcome to Fabulous Las Vegas"

Familiar no doubt from every Las Vegas movie or TV show you've ever seen, the "Welcome to Fabulous Las Vegas" sign is an obligatory photo-op for every visitor, just over half a mile south of Mandalay Bay. To minimize the risk of accidents, only cars heading south, away from the city, can access the narrow patch in between the north- and southbound carriageways of the Strip. Don't try walking this far, least of all in summer.

tropical theming, there's no significance to the name "Mandalay". Instead Mandalay Bay's strongest selling point is its nightlife, with a high-end array of restaurants, bars, clubs – such as *Light* (p.42), the first-ever nightclub to be run under the auspices of Cirque du Soleil – and music venues, including the prestigious *House of Blues* (p.42), plus the self-explanatory Cirque show, Michael Jackson One. To keep its young, affluent guests on site during the day as well, there's also an impressively landscaped network of pools and artificial beaches that includes a wave pool and the "toptional" **Moorea Beach Club**.

Being further south of the Strip's centre of gravity than anyone would choose to walk, Mandalay Bay can feel a little stranded. Forced to work hard to attract and keep visitors, however, it has continued to prosper through the recession. Inevitably, some of its restaurants have lost their original buzz, while the Mandalay Place mall holds little to lure shoppers based elsewhere. For a night out, though, or a weekend in a self-contained luxury resort, Mandalay Bay can still match the best Las Vegas has to offer.

Incidentally, the *Four Seasons* hotel is right here too – its rooms occupy the top five floors of Mandalay Bay's original tower.

SHARK REEF

Mandalay Bay, 3950 Las Vegas Blvd ☎702 632 4555, ⓦsharkreef.com. June–Aug daily 10am–10pm; Sept–May Mon–Thurs & Sun 10am–8pm, Fri & Sat 10am–10pm. Ages 13 and over $18, ages 5–12 $12. MAP P.37, POCKET MAP B8

In keeping with Las Vegas's emphasis on immediate thrills, the **Shark Reef** aquarium focuses almost exclusively on dangerous marine predators, prowling through tanks designed to resemble a decaying ancient temple that's sinking into the sea. The species on show – largely chosen for their scary teeth and deadly stings – include giant crocodiles and Komodo dragons as well, of course, as enormous sharks. Separate eerily illuminated cylindrical tanks are filled with menacing-looking jellyfish.

Shark Reef is located right at the back of Mandalay Bay; to reach it, you have to walk along several hundred yards of internal corridors, beyond the two convention centres.

SHARK REEF

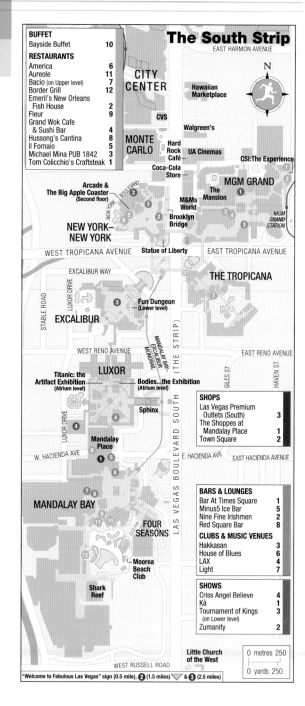

The South Strip

BUFFET

Bayside Buffet	10

RESTAURANTS

America	6
Aureole	11
Bacio (on Upper level)	7
Border Grill	12
Emeril's New Orleans Fish House	2
Fleur	9
Grand Wok Cafe & Sushi Bar	4
Hussong's Cantina	8
Il Fornaio	5
Michael Mina PUB 1842	3
Tom Colicchio's Craftsteak	1

SHOPS

Las Vegas Premium Outlets (South)	3
The Shoppes at Mandalay Place	1
Town Square	2

BARS & LOUNGES

Bar At Times Square	1
Minus5 Ice Bar	5
Nine Fine Irishmen	2
Red Square Bar	8

CLUBS & MUSIC VENUES

Hakkasan	3
House of Blues	6
LAX	4
Light	7

SHOWS

Criss Angel Believe	4
Kà	1
Tournament of Kings (on Lower level)	3
Zumanity	2

EAST HARMON AVENUE

CITY CENTER

Hawaiian Marketplace

CVS

Walgreen's

MONTE CARLO

Hard Rock Café

UA Cinemas

CSI:The Experience

Coca-Cola Store

MGM GRAND

The Mansion

MGM GRAND STATION

Arcade & The Big Apple Coaster (Second floor)

M&Ms World

NEW YORK–NEW YORK

Brooklyn Bridge

Statue of Liberty

WEST TROPICANA AVENUE

EAST TROPICANA AVENUE

EXCALIBUR WAY

THE TROPICANA

STABLE ROAD

LUXOR DRIVE

Fun Dungeon — (Lower level)

EXCALIBUR

WEST RENO AVENUE

EAST RENO AVENUE

MANDALAY BAY / EXCALIBUR MONORAIL

LUXOR

(THE STRIP)

GILES ST

HAVEN ST

Titanic: the Artifact Exhibition (Atrium level)

Bodies...the Exhibition (Atrium level)

Sphinx

LUXOR DRIVE

Mandalay Place

LAS VEGAS BOULEVARD SOUTH

W. HACIENDA AVE

E. HACIENDA AVE

EAST HACIENDA AVENUE

MANDALAY BAY

FOUR SEASONS

Moorea Beach Club

Shark Reef

Little Church of the West

| 0 metres | 250 |
| 0 yards | 250 |

WEST RUSSELL ROAD

"Welcome to Fabulous Las Vegas" sign (0.5 mile), **2** (1.5 miles) ▽ & **3** (2.5 miles)

LUXOR

3900 Las Vegas Blvd S ☎ 702 262 4444, ⓦ luxor.com. MAP P.32, POCKET MAP B6

The huge **Luxor** pyramid, with its sloping, monolithic walls of black shiny glass, was built in 1993 as the follow-up to the much more fanciful Excalibur (see p.34) next door. Originally it was filled to bursting with ancient Egyptian motifs, holding not only a replica of King Tut's tomb but even an indoor River Nile. Then, when Las Vegas (and owners MGM Resorts in particular) decided to gear itself less towards kids and more towards adults, much of Luxor's archeological theming was stripped away. Nothing can mask the fact it's a colossal pyramid, though, and Luxor today seems to be in an odd sort of limbo, embarrassed about its Egyptian past but unable to find an alternative identity.

Visitors who venture this far down the Strip – especially those arriving on the **Mandalay Bay–Excalibur monorail** – still congregate outside to take photos of the enormous Sphinx that straddles the main driveway. Immediately inside the main doors, there's also a re-creation of the facade of the Egyptian temple of Abu Simbel. Beyond that, however, there's little to distinguish the main casino floor. In the absence of noteworthy restaurants or shops, Luxor is best known for its bars and clubs, including an outpost of LA stalwart *LAX* (see p.42).

Immediately upstairs, the so-called Atrium Level, is home to two permanent exhibitions – **Bodies** (see p.34) and **Titanic** – as well as a small food court. It's also the best vantage point from which to admire the pyramid's cavernous interior; only guests can access the higher levels.

LUXOR

TITANIC: THE ARTIFACT EXHIBITION

Atrium Level, Luxor, 3900 Las Vegas Blvd S ☎ 702 262 4400 ⓦ rmstitanic.net. Daily 10am–10pm. $32, ages 4–12 $24, over-64s $30; audio guides $6 extra. MAP P.32, POCKET MAP A5

In an enclosed building upstairs in Luxor, **Titanic: The Artifact Exhibition** is the world's only permanent exhibition of items salvaged from the *Titanic*. Displays that also include mock-ups of the fabled Grand Staircase tell the full story of the great ship, from construction to destruction. Each visitor is invited to pose for a souvenir photo on the Staircase, while as you enter you receive a "boarding pass" named for a specific passenger. Only as you leave do you find out whether he or she survived the catastrophe.

Prize artefacts include the actual wheel at which the helmsman tried and failed to steer clear of the iceberg on April 14, 1912, and the enormous Big Piece, a gigantic slab that broke off C Deck as the ship sank, and was raised from the ocean floor in 1998.

BODIES...THE EXHIBITION

Atrium Level, Luxor, 3900 Las Vegas Blvd S
☎702 262 4400, Ⓦ bodiestheexhibition.com.
Daily 10am–10pm, last admission 9pm. $32,
ages 4–12 $24, over-64s $30; audio guides $6
extra. MAP P.32, POCKET MAP A5

You might expect **Bodies...the Exhibition** to be a gory horror show. In fact, despite the advertising images of goggle-eyed corpses, it provides a surprisingly serious museum-quality experience. You have to keep reminding yourself that what look like brightly coloured mannequins really are dead bodies that have been "plastinated" for permanent display. Some are posed as though in life, playing sports in perpetuity, others have been dissected to show particular features of their anatomy. Certain sections, like that in which an entire circulatory system, down to the tiniest capillary, has been teased out and dyed in different colours, have an astonishing beauty; the sight of fatally diseased organs displayed alongside healthy counterparts are much more sobering. Even if you've wandered in for a quick laugh, you may leave determined to change your life around – not that Las Vegas is necessarily the best place to start.

EXCALIBUR

3850 Las Vegas Blvd S ☎702 597 7777,
Ⓦ excalibur.com. MAP P.32, POCKET MAP B4

Built in 1990, **Excalibur** remains the most visible reminder of the era when Las Vegas briefly re-invented itself as a vast children's playground. With its jam-packed, multi-coloured turrets and ring of clunky battlements it doesn't so much look like a castle, as like a child's drawing of a castle – and to be more specific still, a drawing of Walt Disney's version of Sleeping Beauty's castle. In fact, the architect responsible, Veldon Simpson, who later went on to design both Luxor and the MGM Grand, had travelled around Europe visiting hundreds of real-life castles. He ultimately settled on using the same model that Disney had, Neuschwanstein in Bavaria, a whimsical hybrid of French château and stern German fortress. Only a nit-picker would mention that the original Excalibur was a sword, not a castle.

These days, Excalibur is less child-oriented than it used to be. Its primary function for current owners MGM seems to be as a kind of gateway to draw visitors towards the southern end of the Strip, complementing

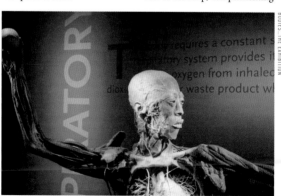

the free monorail to Luxor (see p.33) and Mandalay Bay (p.30), prominent outside, with an easy indoor walkway to those properties further back. You access that by heading onto the upper level from the casino, lured ever onwards down the corridor by boutiques and fast-food places.

As Excalibur generally offers some of the Strip's least expensive hotel rooms, it caters largely to low-budget tour groups and families. That can result in a slightly jarring clash between its remaining child-friendly Arthurian theming, which includes the jousting-and-serving wenches dinner-show *Tournament of Kings* (see p.43), and blue-collar adult entertainment such as *Dick's Last Resort* bar and the *Thunder From Down Under* male stripper revue. Its lowest level, below the casino floor, is occupied by the **Fun Dungeon** (daily 10am–10pm), a jumble of fairground stalls, carnival amusements and arcade games.

Much of the upstairs, officially known as the Castle Walk Level, is taken up by a huge **food court**, which includes a massive *Krispy Kreme* doughnut bakery, where all the kitchen action is open to passers-by, and a *Tropical Smoothie Café* outlet. It's also home to the frankly poor *Excalibur Buffet* and assorted souvenir "shoppes".

THE TROPICANA

THE TROPICANA

3801 Las Vegas Blvd S ☎ 702 739 2222. ☺ www.troplv.com. MAP P.32, POCKET MAP C4
Built in 1957, standing proudly aloof a mile south of the Strip, the **Tropicana** swiftly became a byword for luxury. It was also renowned from the start as being in the pocket of the Mob, and spent twenty years under investigation for "skimming" of casino profits, money laundering and other Mafia-related skullduggery.

Although it's now poised at the country's busiest crossroads, the Tropicana has long struggled to compete with its mighty MGM-owned neighbours – Excalibur (p.34), the MGM Grand (p.37), and New York–New York (p.36). Barely rescued from bankruptcy in 2008, it was given a $125-million makeover intended to restore its tropical-playground image and add something of the feel of Miami's South Beach. Among the casualties of that process was its fabled topless revue, the Folies Bergère, which sadly ended its residency shortly before its fiftieth anniversary.

While it's looking much crisper and brighter than before, the Tropicana still can't match the latest Strip giants. Hopes that it would blossom as a nightlife destination have failed to materialize, and it holds little to draw in sightseers, shoppers or diners. Instead it remains slightly apart, with its strongest feature being an extensive pool complex that's open to guests only.

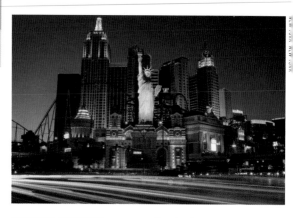

NEW YORK–NEW YORK

3790 Las Vegas Blvd S ☎702 740 6969.
Ⓦnewyorknewyork.com. MAP P.32.
POCKET MAP C3

The first, and arguably the best, of Las Vegas's modern breed of replica "cities", **New York–New York** opened in 1997. Its exterior consists of a squeezed-up, half-sized rendition of the Manhattan skyline as it looked in the 1950s. The interior, which makes no attempt to correspond to the specific "buildings" outside, holds a smaller than average casino, plus a dining and nightlife district intended to evoke Greenwich Village.

Despite the broad Brooklyn Bridge that stretches along the Strip sidewalk, and the Empire State and Chrysler buildings etched against the Nevada sky, the most iconic feature of the facade is the **Statue of Liberty**, facing the intersection with Tropicana Avenue. Unlike the other elements here it's actually twice the height of the real-life statue. This spot never hosted a replica of the World Trade Center, but ad-hoc memorials appeared here after September 11, 2001.

New York–New York has lost much of its original playful theming in recent years. Sightseers once stepped off the Strip to find themselves in Central Park at night, with owls peeping down from the trees. Things are more serious these days, enlivened here and there with stylish Art Deco motifs.

New York–New York isn't served by any monorail, but pedestrians pass through one corner en route between the pedestrian bridges to Excalibur and the MGM Grand. Perhaps to tempt them to stay, the areas nearest the Strip hold an abundance of bars, pubs and food outlets. Much of the second floor is taken up by the Arcade, a rather ramshackle assortment of sideshows, games and kids' attractions.

THE BIG APPLE COASTER

New York–New York, 3790 Las Vegas Blvd S
☎702 740 6969. Ⓦ newyorknewyork.com.
Mon–Thurs & Sun 11am–11pm, Fri & Sat
10.30am–midnight. $14 first ride, $25 for an
all-day Scream Pass. MAP P.32. POCKET MAP B3

From the moment you catch a glimpse of New York–New York, you'll almost certainly also see – and hear – the tiny little yellow cabs that loop and race around its skyscraper towers. Previously known first as the Manhattan Express, then simply as The Roller Coaster, and now re-renamed **The Big Apple Coaster**, it operates from a replica subway station on the casino's upper floor. Speeding at 67mph, plunging over 200ft and rolling like a jet fighter, it's a serious thrill ride no theme-park fan should miss.

MGM GRAND

3799 Las Vegas Blvd S ☎ 702 891 7777, ⊚ mgmgrand.com. MAP P.32, POCKET MAP C3

The enormous **MGM Grand** casino has been through many changes since it opened in 1993. Back then, it attracted huge publicity as the largest hotel in the world and the first to incorporate its own theme park. It was also the location of the legendary boxing fight when Mike Tyson bit Evander Holyfield's ear in 1997.

These days, however, the MGM Grand keeps a lower profile, and it would be hard to say what identity it's aiming for any more. All traces of the theme park have long since vanished, while only the general preponderance of green now recalls the property's initial *Wizard of Oz* theme. With its original 5005 rooms boosted by the addition of the three all-suite *Signature* towers, it's surpassed in size only by the Venetian-Palazzo combination. Only in Las Vegas could such a behemoth seem to blend into the background.

One reason for this may be that with so many guests on site, the MGM Grand simply doesn't need to lure visitors in. It still boasts a fabulous array of dining and entertainment options, which includes the stunning Cirque de Soleil show *Kà*, and the *Joël Robuchon Restaurant*, where the $425 Degustation Menu is said to be the world's most expensive prix-fixe menu.

Over the last few years, MGM Resorts have undertaken a massive overhaul of the Grand that has so far seen more old things disappear than new ones emerge. Casualties have included the live lions previously displayed in a glass enclosure just off the Strip, and the veteran *Studio 54* nightclub.

CSI: THE EXPERIENCE

MGM Grand, 3799 Las Vegas Blvd S ☎ 702 891 5749, ⊚ csiexhibit.com. Daily 9am–9pm, last admission 7.30pm. Ages 12 and over $28, $26 for repeat visits on same day, ages 4–11 $21/$20. MAP P.32, POCKET MAP E2

Set well back from the MGM Grand's Strip entrance, **CSI: The Experience** is perhaps the most enjoyable family attraction in Las Vegas. Trading on the worldwide success of the CSI TV franchise, it enables participants to investigate, and almost certainly solve, fictional murder mysteries.

Each ticket entitles you to solve one of three possible cases, taking roughly an hour to examine the murder scene, test out various hypotheses in the lab, and come up with a solution. Assistants are on hand to help, though you don't interact with any actors.

CSI: THE EXPERIENCE

Shops

LAS VEGAS PREMIUM OUTLETS (SOUTH)

7400 Las Vegas Blvd S ☎ 702 896 5599, ⓦ premiumoutlets.com. Mon–Sat 9am–9pm, Sun 9am–8pm. MAP P.32 & P.95, POCKET MAP C9

The sort of mall you might find beside the highway on the outskirts of any town in America, Las Vegas Premium Outlets (South), 3 miles south of Mandalay Bay, offers no-frills, no-nonsense shopping at Banana Republic, Gap, Nike and the like. For visitors with the use of a car, it's not a bad option for picking up everyday items to take back home. There's a basic fast-food court but no restaurants.

THE SHOPPES AT MANDALAY PLACE

Mandalay Bay, 3930 Las Vegas Blvd S ☎ 702 632 7777, ⓦ mandalaybay.com. Mon–Thurs & Sun 10am–11pm, Fri & Sat 10am–midnight. MAP P.32, POCKET MAP B6

Arranged along the indoor hallway that connects Mandalay Bay with Luxor – a fair walk from the centre of either, and from the monorail too – The Shoppes at Mandalay Place does not rank among Las Vegas's premier shopping malls. Instead, it's a rather haphazard mix of big names such as The Guinness Store, Nike Golf and Frederick's of Hollywood, with smart boutiques, galleries and novelty stores, plus several bars and restaurants.

TOWN SQUARE

6605 Las Vegas Blvd S ☎ 702 269 5001, ⓦ mytownsquarelasvegas.com. Mon–Thurs 10am–9pm, Fri & Sat 10am–10pm, Sun 11am–8pm. MAP P.32 & P.95, POCKET MAP C9

Especially popular with locals who prefer to steer clear of the Strip, Town Square, 3 miles south of Mandalay Bay, is a rarity in Las Vegas, designed to be experienced as an outdoor "neighbourhood" rather than an air-conditioned enclave. Visitors from further afield may be less enthused by its attempt to evoke the feel of a "European village". Big stores include Staples, a Whole Foods supermarket and an Apple Store that offers free wi-fi; there are also some unremarkable restaurants and a cinema.

Buffet

BAYSIDE BUFFET

Mandalay Bay, 3950 Las Vegas Blvd S ☎ 702 632 7402, ⓦ mandalaybay.com. Mon–Fri 7–11am $18, 11am–2.30pm $22, 4.30–9.45pm $33; Sat & Sun 7am–2.30pm $26 & 4.30–9.45pm $33. MAP P.32, POCKET MAP B7

Mandalay Bay's buffet has a much nicer setting than most of its Las Vegas rivals, overlooking the resort's pool and open, when weather permits, to breezes. Apart from the wide range of desserts, though, and the pre-cut deli sandwiches at lunchtime, the food is not all that amazing.

Restaurants

AMERICA

New York–New York, 3790 Las Vegas Blvd S
☎ 702 740 6451, ⓦ newyorknewyork.com.
Daily 24hr. MAP P.32, POCKET MAP B3

While serious foodies will find
nothing remarkable about this
24-hour diner, it's a great place
to bring kids, or Las Vegas
first-timers, thanks to the
colossal, cartoon-like relief map
of the USA that hangs from the
ceiling. Serving signature dishes
from all over the country, from
Alaskan salmon salad ($16) to
Kansas City ribs ($25), there's
food to match every appetite.

AUREOLE

Mandalay Bay, 3950 Las Vegas Blvd S ☎ 702
632 7200, ⓦ aureolelv.com. Mon–Sat
5.30–10.30pm. MAP P.32, POCKET MAP B7

With its astonishing "wine
tower", a 42ft vertical wine
cellar that's accessed by flying,
white-clad "wine angels", Chef
Charlie Palmer's showcase
restaurant is a real must-see.
His contemporary American
cooking is something special,
best sampled on the set menus
at $85 and $110, costing $10
extra in the smoochy Swan
Court section.

BACIO

Tropicana, 3801 Las Vegas Blvd S ☎ 800 462
8767, ⓦ www.troplv.com. Daily 5–10.30pm.
MAP P.32, POCKET MAP C4

Carla Pellegrino's classic Italian
diner has been a big hit at the
revamped Tropicana, not least
for its dazzling bright-white
styling. The speciality veal chop
costs over $40, but you can get
fresh pasta with marinara sauce
for $22, and the early-evening
set tasting menu offers four
courses with wine for $39.
The one drawback can be
occasionally slow service.

BORDER GRILL

Mandalay Bay, 3950 Las Vegas Blvd S ☎ 702
632 7403, ⓦ www.bordergrill.com. Mon–Thurs
11am–10pm, Fri 11am–11pm, Sat 10am–11pm,
Sun 10am–10pm. MAP P.32, POCKET MAP B8

Serving light and zestful
"modern Mexican" cuisine
that's a perfect match for its
sun-kissed indoor-outdoor
setting, this poolside veteran
serves lunchtime salads, tacos
and *tortas* (flatbreads) for well
under $20, and larger dinner
plates like Yucatan pork for $24
or *mole* roasted chicken for
$28. A three-course set dinner
costs $42 and the hugely
popular weekend brunch $35.

EMERIL'S NEW ORLEANS FISH HOUSE

MGM Grand, 3799 Las Vegas Blvd S ☎ 702
891 7374; ⓦ emerils.com. Daily 11.30am–
10pm. MAP P.32, POCKET MAP E2

Rich New Orleans flavours in
a modern setting, courtesy of
TV chef Emeril Lagasse. As the
name suggests, the emphasis is
on seafood, with barbecue
shrimp as an appetizer ($17)
and pecan-crusted redfish as a
main course ($17), but you can
also get seared chicken or a
rib-eye steak. If you don't have a
dinner reservation, they should
be able to seat you after 9pm.

FLEUR

Mandalay Bay, 3950 Las Vegas Blvd S ☎702 632 7200, ⓦmandalaybay.com. Daily 11am–10.30pm. MAP P.32, POCKET MAP B7

There's much more to Hubert Keller's modern tapas restaurant than its notorious $5000 foie gras burger. Its sumptuous menu features exquisite dishes from all over the world, including Spanish-style grilled octopus ($18) and Greek herb-roasted leg of lamb ($42). Even the so-called "Large Plates" are pretty small, though, so it's no place to be counting your pennies. Parties of four can "Tour the World" for $275.

GRAND WOK & SUSHI BAR

MGM Grand, 3799 Las Vegas Blvd S ⓦmgmgrand.com. Mon–Thurs & Sun 11am–10pm, Fri & Sat 11am–1am. No reservations. MAP P.32, POCKET MAP D3

This pan-Asian restaurant is the kind of place you wish you could find everywhere in Las Vegas. The prices are low, the service fast, the decor fancy enough to make you feel you're somewhere special and they only take walk-ins. And the food? That's great too, drawing on Vietnamese, Thai, Chinese and Japanese. Dim sum and sushi plates cost around $12, and mains more like $20.

HUSSONG'S CANTINA

Mandalay Bay, 3930 Las Vegas Blvd S ☎702 632 6450, ⓦhussongslasvegas.com. Daily 11am–11pm. MAP P.32, POCKET MAP B6

An outpost of the Mexican original that's said to have invented the margarita, *Hussong's* is as much a bar as a restaurant. Don't let that put you off the food, though – it's surprisingly good, with $15–20 flautas, fajitas and chimichangas in case you're hungry for more than the $12 nachos. Don't miss the $6 plazero corn, dusted with cheese flakes.

IL FORNAIO

New York–New York, 3790 Las Vegas Blvd S ☎702 650 6500, ⓦilfornaio.com /lasvegas. Restaurant Mon–Thurs & Sun 7.30am–midnight, Fri & Sat 7.30am–1am; Panetteria daily 6am–5.30pm. MAP P.32, POCKET MAP B3

While *Il Fornaio* is open for decent Italian food pretty much round the clock, in-the-know locals love it best of all in the morning, when you can enjoy a wonderful sit-down breakfast or simply pop in to the separate deli/bakery next door for fresh breads and espresso coffee.

MICHAEL MINA PUB 1842

MGM Grand, 3799 Las Vegas Blvd S ☎702 891 3922; ⓦmgmgrand.com. Mon, Thurs & Sun 11.30am–10pm, Fri & Sat 11.30am–11pm. MAP P.32, POCKET MAP D3

Top Las Vegas chef Michael Mina keeps things simple with his take on the gastro pub, serving substantial $18–22 burgers and old-fashioned favourites like fish and chips ($26) or succulent St Louis ribs ($22/34), along with $8–11 Happy-Hour "small plates" like brisket sliders or lobster grilled cheese and a couple of dozen draft beers.

IL FORNAIO

TOM COLICCHIO'S CRAFTSTEAK

MGM Grand, 3799 Las Vegas Blvd S ☎ 702 891 7318; ⊛ mgmgrand.com. Mon–Thurs & Sun 5.30–10pm, Fri & Sat 5.30–10.30pm. MAP P.32, POCKET MAP E2

Serious carnivores swear this dinner-only steakhouse serves the best beef in Las Vegas, in melt-in-your-mouth inch-thick cuts. Order à la carte, with lobster bisque ($18) as an appetizer and steaks from $36. Set menus range from $119 for domestic Angus beef to $295 for wagyu surf & turf.

Bars and lounges

MINUS5 ICE BAR

BAR AT TIMES SQUARE

New York–New York, 3790 Las Vegas Blvd S ☎ 702 740 6466, ⊛ newyorknewyork.com. Daily 11am–2.30am, showtime 8pm–2am. Cover $10 standing, reserved seating Mon–Thurs & Sun $15, Fri & Sat $25. MAP P.32, POCKET MAP B3

If you like your nights out sophisticated or edgy, steer clear of this raucous sing-a-long bar alongside New York–New York's main casino floor; if you prefer to scream along at the top of your voice as two pianists go head-to-head, playing whatever requests spring to their tipsy audience's mind, you're in the right place.

MINUS5 ICE BAR

Mandalay Bay, 3930 Las Vegas Blvd S ☎ 702 740 5800, ⊛ www.minus5experience.com. Mon–Thurs & Sun 11am–2am, Fri & Sat 11am–3am. Cover varies, typically $25 including 1 drink. MAP P.32, POCKET MAP B6

This funny, gimmicky Mandalay Place bar is exactly what it says it is – every single thing is made of ice, from walls to glasses, though at least the couches are spread with deer skins. Customers are loaned jackets, gloves and boots to tolerate the temperature – yes, it's minus 5.

NINE FINE IRISHMEN

New York–New York, 3790 Las Vegas Blvd S ☎ 702 740 6463, ⊛ ninefineirishmen.com. Daily 11am–2.45am. Cover $5 Wed & Thurs, $10 Fri & Sat. MAP P.32, POCKET MAP C3

A genuine Irish pub, shipped in pieces from Ireland, celebrating Irish beer, food and, in the evening, music and dance too. A small patio out on the Strip looks over "Brooklyn Bridge". During the weekday Happy Hour (Mon–Thurs 2–5pm), Guinness and other beers cost $5 per pint.

RED SQUARE BAR

Mandalay Bay, 3950 Las Vegas Blvd S ☎ 702 632 7407, ⊛ mandalaybay.com. Mon–Thurs 4pm–1am, Fri & Sat 4pm–2am, Sun 1pm–1am. MAP P.32, POCKET MAP B7

Both a bar and a restaurant, *Red Square* is designed to evoke all things Russian – the decadence of the Tsars, the graphic style of the Communist era and the icy chill of the steppes. Unless you have a real penchant for caviar, the food is a bit too expensive to be worth it, but the bar is great, with its solid-ice counter-top and frozen vodka vault.

Clubs and music venues

HOUSE OF BLUES

HAKKASAN

MGM Grand, 3799 Las Vegas Blvd S ☎702 891 3838, ⓦ hakkasanlv.com. Thurs, Fri & Sun 10pm–dawn, Sat 9pm– dawn. Cover men $20, women $10. MAP 32, POCKET MAP D3

Said to be the largest club in the world, an offshoot of what was originally a Chinese restaurant in London, this colossal, multi-level place incorporates two separate full-sized nightclubs, plus all sorts of dining rooms, ultra-lounges and private gardens; superstar DJs attract up to 7500 clubbers at weekends.

HOUSE OF BLUES

Mandalay Bay, 3950 Las Vegas Blvd S ☎702 632 7600, ⓦ www.houseofblues.com. Mon–Thurs & Sun 8am–11pm, Fri & Sat 8am–midnight. MAP P.32, POCKET MAP B6

The national *House of Blues* music chain has recently revamped its Las Vegas outlet, in the heart of Mandalay Bay. While retaining its funky, voodoo-esque feel, the capacity has been reduced to a more intimate 1300. Individual concerts are interspersed with longer artist residencies; thus Carlos Santana has been signed up for regular long-term stints, with ticket prices from $89.

LAX

Luxor, 3900 Las Vegas Blvd S ☎702 262 4529, ⓦ luxor.com. Thurs–Sat 10pm–4am. Cover men $30, women $20. MAP P.32, POCKET MAP B6

This offshoot of Hollywood's hot *LAX* nightclub can be a victim of its own success; the whole place, from the dramatic staircase to the long dance floor, gets way too crowded for comfort on big nights. If money is no object, skip the queues by paying for VIP table service. If you're happy with the mainstream music choices it's up there with Las Vegas's best.

LIGHT

Mandalay Bay, 3950 Las Vegas Blvd S ☎702 588 5656, ⓦ thelightvegas.com. Wed 10.30pm–4am, Fri & Sat 10pm–4am. Cover charge varies. MAP P.32, POCKET MAP B7

Mandalay Bay has pulled off a real coup by hosting the first-ever Cirque du Soleil nightclub, designed to keep visitors to *Michael Jackson One* dancing all night. Holding over two thousand clubbers, it features a mobile DJ booth that rises from the floor, plus live Cirque performers. In summer, the beachclub *Daylight* (ⓦ daylight-vegas.com) stages outdoor pool parties and evening concerts.

Shows

CRISS ANGEL BELIEVE

Luxor, 3900 Las Vegas Blvd S ☎702 262 4400, ⓦ luxor.com. Tues, Thurs & Sat 7pm & 9.30pm, Wed & Fri 7pm. $65–143. MAP P.32, POCKET MAP A6

Believe bears the Cirque brand, but beyond the odd animal cost-ume it's no longer really targeted at Cirque fans. Instead it's a showcase for everything Angel does best, blending close-up trickery with mind-blowing illusions to become the city's most exciting magic show. See past the pyrotechnics and blaring heavy metal, and Angel is a surprisingly old-fashioned performer who wins over his audience night after night.

KÀ

MGM Grand, 3799 Las Vegas Blvd S ☎702 531 3826, ⓦcirquedusoleil.com. Mon–Wed, Sat & Sun 7pm & 9.30pm. $69–180. MAP P.32, POCKET MAP D2

There's more martial-arts musclery to the Cirque du Soleil's MGM Grand spectacular than to the company's more ethereal offerings; even sceptics are guaranteed to find the set-piece stunts enacted on its tilting, rotating stage absolutely jaw-dropping. Add in some extraordinary puppetry and sumptuous costumes, and while the twins-in-jeopardy storyline may leave you unmoved, *Kà* is certain to expand your horizons.

TOURNAMENT OF KINGS

Excalibur, 3850 Las Vegas Blvd S ☎702 597 7600, ⓦexcalibur.com. Mon & Fri 6pm, Wed, Thurs, Sat & Sun 6pm & 8.30pm. $66 including dinner. MAP P.32, POCKET MAP A4

Excalibur's swashbuckling swords-and-slapstick supper show plunges family audiences back to "the Olden Days" to participate in a medieval jousting contest, complete with villainous black knights and maidens in peril. If you'd rather eat chicken with your fingers than sit through Shakespeare, this is the show for you.

ZUMANITY

New York–New York, 3790 Las Vegas Blvd S ☎702 740 6815, ⓦcirquedusoleil.com. Tues–Sat 7pm & 9.30pm. $69–105, or $125 per person for a "duo sofa". All shows over-18s only. MAP P.32, POCKET MAP B3

Cirque rule the roost in Las Vegas these days and this show contains enough of their trademark flair for acrobatics to remind you why. However, while the concept – Cirque goes sexy – may pique your curiosity, the reality is disappointing. What's most surprising is how it undercuts the erotic potential of fit bodies performing astonishing feats with pratfalls and smut. At times, it looks amazing, but it's no substitute for Cirque at their peak.

Wedding chapel

LITTLE CHURCH OF THE WEST

4617 Las Vegas Blvd S ☎ 702 739 7971, ⓦlittlechurchlv.com. Daily 8am–11pm. MAP P.32, POCKET MAP C9

Oddly enough, this cute little chapel really is old, at least by Las Vegas standards, having been built for the Last Frontier casino in 1942 and migrated down the Strip to its current location, half a mile south of Mandalay Bay. With its tranquil garden, it feels a world away from the big-casino chapels. Packages range from the $199 "Let's Elope" to the $2975 "Unforgettable VIP Package".

LITTLE CHURCH OF THE WEST

CityCenter and around

When MGM Resorts opened the CityCenter complex, in 2009, the aim was to add a whole new neighbourhood to Las Vegas, giving the city a new kind of sleek, corporate architecture. By building a self-contained enclave set back from the Strip, they would vastly increase the value of what was previously unused land, and finally make it possible to expand east–west. A massive financial gamble, the project involved a huge new casino, Aria; a high-end shopping mall, Crystals; and several hotel-and-condo skyscrapers. A new neighbourhood has indeed appeared, at each end of which MGM have cannily integrated an older Strip-front casino – Monte Carlo to the south and Bellagio to the north. The one fly in the ointment is the brash new Cosmopolitan, cheekily added to the one tiny speck of Strip real estate that MGM didn't own.

MONTE CARLO

3770 Las Vegas Blvd S ☎702 730 7777, ⓦmontecarlo.com. MAP P.45, POCKET MAP C2

Named for Monaco's world-famous gambling destination, the low-profile **Monte Carlo** ranked for many years among Las Vegas's least showy casinos. Since the unveiling of CityCenter, however, it has acquired a new prominence as the southern gateway to the CityCenter complex. Eye-catching indoor-outdoor attractions including the all-American Double Barrel Roadhouse, and *Diablo's Cantina*, a lively Mexican bar, are now arrayed along its frontage in the hope of luring pedestrians in off the Strip who will then keep walking all the way back to Aria.

Although a futuristic **monorail** system connects the Monte Carlo to Bellagio by way of Aria, it's so far back from the Strip, at either end, that its only significance is as a free fun ride.

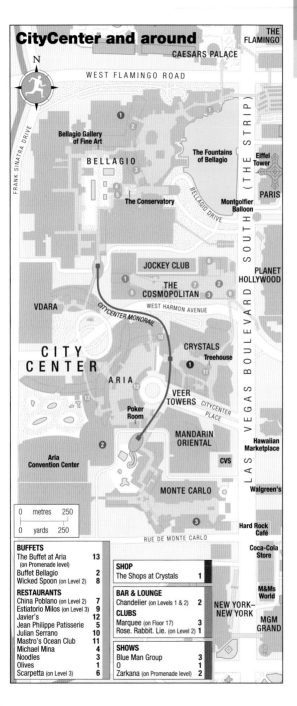

CityCenter and around

THE FLAMINGO

CAESARS PALACE

WEST FLAMINGO ROAD

N

Bellagio Gallery of Fine Art

BELLAGIO

The Fountains of Bellagio

Eiffel Tower

The Conservatory

PARIS

Montgolfier Balloon

FRANK SINATRA DRIVE

BELLAGIO DRIVE

JOCKEY CLUB

PLANET HOLLYWOOD

THE **COSMOPOLITAN**

WEST HARMON AVENUE

SOUTH (THE STRIP)

VDARA

CITYCENTER MONORAIL

CITY CENTER

CRYSTALS

Treehouse

ARIA

VEER TOWERS

CITYCENTER PLACE

Poker Room

MANDARIN ORIENTAL

Hawaiian Marketplace

Aria Convention Center

CVS

LAS VEGAS BOULEVARD

MONTE CARLO

Walgreen's

Hard Rock Café

RUE DE MONTE CARLO

Coca-Cola Store

| 0 | metres | 250 |
| 0 | yards | 250 |

M&Ms World

NEW YORK– NEW YORK

MGM GRAND

BUFFETS

The Buffet at Aria (on Promenade level)	13
Buffet Bellagio	2
Wicked Spoon (on Level 2)	8

RESTAURANTS

China Poblano (on Level 2)	7
Estiatorio Milos (on Level 3)	9
Javier's	12
Jean Philippe Patisserie	5
Julian Serrano	10
Mastro's Ocean Club	11
Michael Mina	4
Noodles	3
Olives	1
Scarpetta (on Level 3)	6

SHOP

| The Shops at Crystals | 1 |

BAR & LOUNGE

| Chandelier (on Levels 1 & 2) | 2 |

CLUBS

| Marquee (on Floor 17) | 3 |
| Rose. Rabbit. Lie. (on Level 2) | 1 |

SHOWS

| Blue Man Group | 3 |
| Zarkana (on Promenade level) | 2 |

45

CRYSTALS

CRYSTALS

3720 Las Vegas Blvd S ☎702 590 9299, Ⓦtheshopsatcrystals.com. MAP P.45, POCKET MAP B1 & F9

As the one public component of CityCenter to abut the Strip, **Crystals** certainly catches the eye. Designed by Daniel Libeskind, its jagged, colourful facade makes a contrast with the white walls and air-conditioned cool of its interior. Its primary role is as a (hugely expensive) shopping mall, **The Shops at Crystals** (see p.50).

Purely as a spectacle, however, Crystals is well worth a quick walk-through. At one point, it was planned as an urban park, and it features some extravagant, playful wooden structures, including the intricate 70ft **Treehouse**, home to the stylish *Mastro's Ocean Club* restaurant (see p.51), as well as a pair of arching wooden "pods".

There's also plenty of water on show, including the swirling glass-encased **fountains** on the lower floor, and some dazzling **sculptures** of neon light.

THE COSMOPOLITAN

3708 Las Vegas Blvd S ☎702 698 7000, Ⓦwww.cosmopolitanlasvegas.com. MAP P.45, POCKET MAP F9

At first glance, most Las Vegas visitors assume that **The Cosmopolitan**, facing Planet Hollywood (see p.54) across the Strip, is just one more piece of the modernist jigsaw puzzle that comprises CityCenter. It's not; it's an entirely separate luxury casino-hotel, stacked up vertically rather than sprawling horizontally, and impishly squeezed atop the former Jockey Club car park, slap in front of CityCenter, which MGM never managed to buy up.

Since opening in 2010, the Cosmopolitan has made itself very much at home in this prime spot, seducing locals and tourists alike with its glitzy architectural flourishes, high-profile **Marquee** nightclub (see p.53), excellent array of appealing restaurants just steps away from the Strip, and general evocation of glamorous days gone by. In the evenings especially, its buzzing public spaces tend to jostle with excited crowds.

The Cosmopolitan is a throwback to the old Las Vegas, when each casino was separately owned and run, acted like the rest of the city didn't exist, saw its business as being all about gambling and nightlife rather than shopping, and aimed to keep visitors on site by making it all but impossible to find the exits. Be warned that the Cosmopolitan also has the last laugh on CityCenter: while you might understandably assume that you could simply walk all the way through the building and reach Aria (see p.47), you can't – there's no pedestrian through route.

ARIA

3730 Las Vegas Blvd S ☎702 590 7111, 🌐www.aria.com. MAP P.45, POCKET MAP B1

Although the CityCenter "neighbourhood" is supposed to be easy to explore on foot, you're only likely to visit **Aria**, the casino at its heart, if you make a very deliberate effort to reach it. Pedestrians can get here outdoors by following its hot, exposed approach road 250yd west from the Strip, or more comfortably indoors, via the Crystals mall or the much longer walkways through Bellagio (see p.48) and the Monte Carlo (see p.44). A gleaming sci-fi **monorail** also connects Aria with both those properties, but the stations are so far back from the Strip that you gain very little by using it.

From the outside, with its sleek, curving skyscrapers, Aria looks more like a sophisticated big-city corporate HQ than a casino. The traffic circle in front of its main entrance holds a pulsating **fountain**, while to the left, more water cascades down a sleek, glistening black wall, 24ft tall.

Aria also identifies itself more with, say, Chicago than Las Vegas by eschewing billboards, video screens and neon in favour of prestigious **contemporary art**. Sculptors represented include Henry Moore, one of whose signature abstractions stands in the tiny gap between Aria and Crystals; Claes Oldenburg, responsible for the giant typewriter eraser near the Strip; Antony Gormley, whose *Feeling Material* hangs from the ceiling; and Maya Lin, whose 84ft silver casting of the Colorado River stretches above the check-in desks.

While Aria's dazzling modernism certainly makes a welcome contrast with traditional Las Vegas aesthetics, in the end, of course, it's all in the service of Mammon – and more specifically, gambling. There's plenty more cutting-edge design to admire as you walk through the casino proper – don't miss the **Poker Room** fringed by gigantic golden playing cards – but there's little reason to linger unless your intention is to gamble.

Both the upper and lower levels of Aria hold a fine roster of restaurants, bars and cafés, but there are very few shops. Devoid of slots and gaming tables, the upper level can feel cavernously empty unless the **Convention Center** is in full swing.

When Aria opened it was home to a Cirque du Soleil tribute show to Elvis Presley. Always an unlikely fit for such a forward-looking property, the show ended its run in 2012 and has since been replaced by a more generic Cirque production, **Zarkana** (see p.53), which had already toured overseas.

ARIA

BELLAGIO

3600 Las Vegas Blvd S ☎ 702 693 7111, ⓦ bellagio.com. MAP P.45, POCKET MAP F7

Ranking high among Las Vegas's absolute must-see casinos, **Bellagio** proudly surveys the Strip across the graceful dancing fountains of its own broad, semicircular lake. This cream-coloured vision of Italian elegance was unveiled in 1998 as the final great flourish of the twentieth century's fastest-growing new city. It was the handiwork of legendary entrepreneur Steve Wynn, who spared no expense in his bid to follow his success with the Mirage (see p.68) by building the greatest hotel the world had ever seen. His original idea was to model it on a French Mediterranean beach and call it Beau Rivage; that changed after he visited the village of Bellagio, beside Lake Como in Italy.

Although Wynn himself is no longer at the helm – when MGM bought out his Mirage corporation in 2000, he took the money and ran down the street to start again – Bellagio is still going strong, racking up the highest turnover and biggest profits in the city. It's also larger than ever, having thrust a tentacle southwards to create an indoor walkway down to CityCenter. As Bellagio's northeast corner is just a few steps across a pedestrian bridge from Caesars Palace (see p.58), many sightseers use it as a corridor to stay out of the sun as they head south, creating a constant flow of visitors.

Almost all of Bellagio's Strip facade is taken up with waterfront restaurants, so once you're inside you won't see much of the lake. Similarly, its colonnaded pool area is only open to guests. Even so, the sheer opulence of the main casino floor is astounding, and several of the public areas should not be missed. In addition to the **Conservatory**, be sure to walk through the hotel lobby, where a vast chandelier of multi-coloured glass flowers, created by sculptor Dale Chihuly, swarms across the ceiling. And take a glance behind the check-in counter to see the Roman gardens accessible to employees only.

When Bellagio first opened, the management briefly attempted to impose a dress code and bar the children of non-guests. Las Vegas's democratic open-to-all traditions soon put paid to that policy, however, so there's

BELLAGIO

nothing snooty about the crowds you'll see window-shopping in the exclusive stores of the small Via Bellagio shopping arcade, or gasping at the menu prices for its magnificent but undeniably expensive restaurants. Other than the building itself, the two most popular attractions that bring in visitors from elsewhere are the **buffet** (see p.50) and Cirque du Soleil's long-running, breathtaking water spectacular, **O** (see p.53).

THE CONSERVATORY

THE FOUNTAINS OF BELLAGIO

Bellagio, 3600 Las Vegas Blvd S. Mon–Fri 3–8pm every 30min, 8pm–midnight every 15min; Sat noon–8pm every 30min, 8pm–midnight every 15min; Sun 11am–3pm every 15min, 3–8pm every 30min, 8pm–midnight every 15min. Free. MAP P.45, POCKET MAP F7

Even when it's lying dormant, Bellagio's ice-blue eight-acre lake makes an impressive spectacle in the Nevada desert. When it erupts into a balletic extravaganza of jetting **fountains**, as it does from early morning/afternoon until midnight daily, it's the best free show in town. The sky-high spurts and streams are accompanied by booming music – mostly songs from Broadway shows and popular classics. For anyone other than diners in the expensive waterfront restaurants the best views are either from the Strip sidewalk (stake your place early), from the top of the Eiffel Tower in Paris (see p.57) or from the guest rooms in either Paris (see p.118) or the Cosmopolitan (see p.115).

THE CONSERVATORY

Bellagio, 3600 Las Vegas Blvd S. Open 24hr. Free. MAP P.45, POCKET MAP E8

Ever since Bellagio opened, its magnificent **Conservatory** has been considered one of the major sights of the city. A glassed-over courtyard ringed by galleries and restaurants, it's repeatedly transformed by a huge team of gardeners into extravagant themed shows that include bizarre whimsical props amid an extraordinary array of living plants. The five separate seasonal displays start with the Chinese New Year and then celebrate spring, summer, autumn and winter. During the week it takes to dismantle each show and prepare the next, there's nothing to see.

BELLAGIO GALLERY OF FINE ART

Bellagio, 3600 Las Vegas Blvd S ☎ 702 693 7871, ⦿ bellagio.com. Daily 10am–8pm. $15. MAP P.45, POCKET MAP E7

Originally home to Steve Wynn's own art collection, the **Bellagio Gallery of Fine Art** managed to survive Wynn's departure and continues to put on changing exhibitions that generally last for around six months. The entrance fee is high for such a small space though, and only worth paying for the better shows, such as the 2012–13 display of twenty paintings by Claude Monet, which was curated in conjunction with the Museum of Fine Arts in Boston.

THE SHOPS AT CRYSTALS

Pay $13 extra for unlimited beer, wine, champagne or Bloody Marys. An entire lobster is served at your table during weekend dinners.

BUFFET BELLAGIO

Bellagio, 3600 Las Vegas Blvd S ☎702 791 7111, 🌐bellagio.com. Breakfast Mon–Fri 7–11am $19; lunch Mon–Fri 11am–3.30pm $23; brunch Sat & Sun 7am–3.30pm $30 (or $42 with champagne); dinner daily 3.30–10pm, Mon–Thurs & Sun $34, Fri & Sat $40. MAP P.45, POCKET MAP E7

The first "gourmet buffet" in town sparked standards, and less happily prices, to rise all over Las Vegas. While no longer quite as exceptional, it still features an amazing array of food; even for breakfast you can have salmon smoked or baked and omelettes cooked to order, with fillings such as crabmeat.

WICKED SPOON

Level 2, The Cosmopolitan, 3708 Las Vegas Blvd S ☎702 698 7000, 🌐www.cosmopolitan lasvegas.com. Brunch Mon–Thurs 8am–2pm $27, Fri–Sun 8am–3pm $35; dinner Mon–Thurs 5–9pm $38; Fri & Sat 3–10pm $41; Sun 3–9pm $41. MAP P.45, POCKET MAP J6

Although the Cosmopolitan's buffet is hard to find, right at the back upstairs, plenty of visitors make their way here to enjoy a wide range of carefully prepared cuisines. Most are served as individual portions, though you can take as many as you like. There's no breakfast; fill up with a late-morning brunch instead.

Shop

THE SHOPS AT CRYSTALS

3720 Las Vegas Blvd S ☎702 590 5299, 🌐theshopsatcrystals.com. Mon–Thurs & Sun 10am–11pm, Fri & Sat 10am–midnight. MAP P.45, POCKET MAP F9

Pitched at Las Vegas's proverbial "whales"– high-rolling big spenders – the glitzy Shops at Crystals makes no bones about being very high-end indeed. With its sparkling white walls, and exquisite sculptural features, few dare stray into boutiques belonging to designers such as Paul Smith and Stella McCartney.

Buffets

THE BUFFET AT ARIA

Promenade Level. Aria, 3730 Las Vegas Blvd S ☎702 590 7111, 🌐aria.com. Breakfast Mon–Fri 7–11am $20; lunch Mon–Fri 11am–3.30pm $24; brunch Sat & Sun 7am–3.30pm $30; dinner daily 3.30–10pm, Mon–Thurs $35, Fri–Sun $40. MAP P.45, POCKET MAP A2

Choices at CityCenter's one buffet are more limited than elsewhere, but the food is a cut above. The sushi and Indian specialities are excellent and the desserts are the best in town.

Restaurants

CHINA POBLANO

Level 2, The Cosmopolitan, 3708 Las Vegas Blvd S ☎702 698 7900, 🌐chinapoblano.com. Daily 11.30am–11.30pm. MAP P.45, POCKET MAP K6

The concept of combining Asia and Mexico goes back a long way – *china poblana* is the national dress of Mexico. Here, in what looks like a street café, it's Chinese and Mexican cuisines that are blended. Only a few dishes, like the $18 Huitlacoche noodles, literally mix the two, but picking and choosing you can make yourself an interesting, good-value meal.

ESTIATORIO MILOS

Level 3, The Cosmopolitan, 3708 Las Vegas Blvd S 🕾 702 698 7930, ⓦ milos.ca. Mon–Thurs 5.30–11.30pm, Fri 5.30pm–midnight, Sat noon–2.30pm & 5.30pm–midnight, Sun noon–2.30pm & 5.30–11pm. MAP P.45, POCKET MAP K7

Vast urns and exquisite statues adorn this beautiful Greek restaurant. For lunch there's a fantastic $22 set menu; in the evening your choice from the tempting array of fresh fish, flown in daily from Athens, will arrive at your table cooked to perfection, and cost around $50 per person.

JAVIER'S

Casino Level, Aria, 3730 Las Vegas Blvd S 🕾 866 590 3637, ⓦ aria.com. Daily 10.30am–midnight. MAP P.45, POCKET MAP B1

Spectacular Mexican restaurant, complete with terrifying wooden carvings, that serves all the standard dishes, scrupulously prepared, for around $20 – a build-your-own-tacos plate for two costs $40 – as well as inventive variations like lobster enchiladas for $25, and shrimp, steak and seafood mains at up to $50.

JEAN PHILIPPE PATISSERIE

Bellagio, 3600 Las Vegas Blvd S ⓦ jpchocolates .com. Mon–Thurs 6am–11pm, Fri–Sun 6am–midnight. No reservations. MAP P.45, POCKET MAP E8

It takes rare self-discipline to walk past Jean-Philippe Maury's extraordinary bakery without pausing to swoon at its central feature; the world's largest chocolate fountain swirls around the entire room, cascading through endless funnels and pipettes. The urge to stop for a $5 mug of hot chocolate, if not a pastry, is all but overwhelming.

JULIAN SERRANO

Casino Level, Aria, 3730 Las Vegas Blvd S 🕾 877 230 2742, ⓦ aria.com. Mon–Thurs & Sun 11.30am–11pm, Fri & Sat 11.30am–11.30pm. MAP P.45, POCKET MAP F9

One of Las Vegas's biggest hits of recent years, this beautiful tapas bar tastes even better than it looks. Most tapas cost $12–15 for a small portion; be sure to branch out and sample fabulous creations like the cocoa butter balls filled with chilled gazpacho. Larger mains include paella for two from $40.

MASTRO'S OCEAN CLUB

Crystals, 3720 Las Vegas Blvd S 🕾 702 798 7115, ⓦ www.mastrosrestaurants.com. Daily 5–11pm. MAP P.45, POCKET MAP B1

Even the new Las Vegas still has a penchant for a good old-fashioned steakhouse, though this one stands out from the crowd not so much for its heavy-duty $50-plus rib-eyes as its amazing setting; reserve early and you get to dine in the bowers of Crystals' whimsical wooden Treehouse.

JEAN PHILIPPE PATISSERIE

MICHAEL MINA

Bellagio, 3600 Las Vegas Blvd S ☎ 702 693 7223, Ⓦ www.michaelmina.net. Daily except Wed 5.30–10pm. MAP P.45, POCKET MAP E8

In his flagship restaurant adjoining Bellagio's Conservatory, Egyptian-born Michael Mina continues to reinvent his tried and tested classics. Starters like tuna tartare with mint cost up to $28, while mains range from $42 to the $55 filo-dusted Dover sole and Mina's signature lobster pot pie. The chef's tasting menu costs $115 (wine pairings $65 extra); there's a no-choice vegetarian menu for $85; and at 5.30pm or 6pm you can enjoy a $65 pre-theatre menu.

NOODLES

Bellagio, 3600 Las Vegas Blvd S ☎ 702 693 8131, Ⓦ bellagio.com. Daily 11am–2am. MAP P.45, POCKET MAP F8

Bellagio's casual, walk-ins only, pan-Asian diner, off the main casino floor behind the *Baccarat* bar, is well worth seeking out. Its intriguing decor looks great and the food, ranging from Thailand to Japan by way of China and Vietnam, is no disappointment. Noodle dishes are around $18 and at weekend lunchtimes dim sum typically cost around $9.

OLIVES

Bellagio, 3600 Las Vegas Blvd S ☎ 702 693 8865, Ⓦ bellagio.com. Daily 11am–2.45pm & 5–10.30pm. MAP P.45, POCKET MAP F7

This elegant modern American restaurant offers an experience to savour. For a light meal, opt for an $18 flatbread topped perhaps with fig and prosciutto. Full mains tend to be pricier, with pasta dishes at over $40 and steaks over $50, but the succulent roasted chicken costs $22 at lunch, $29 for dinner.

SCARPETTA

Level 3, The Cosmopolitan, 3708 Las Vegas Blvd S ☎ 877 893 2003, Ⓦ www.cosmopolitanlasvegas.com. Daily 6–11pm. MAP P.45, POCKET MAP K7

Courtesy of "new Italian" chef Scott Conant, the food is even better than the view at *Scarpetta,* with huge panoramic windows overlooking the Bellagio fountains. *Le tout* Las Vegas has flocked to enjoy starters like his $18 tuna "susci", and mains including short rib and bone marrow agnolotti (stuffed pasta; $25). For the full works, go for the $110 set menu.

Bars and lounges

CHANDELIER

Cosmopolitan, 3708 Las Vegas Blvd S ☎ 702 698 7000, Ⓦ www.cosmopolitanlasvegas.com. Casino level open 24hr, other levels hours vary. MAP P.45, POCKET MAP K6 & F9

Beneath the dazzling, dangling canopy of the eponymous two-million-crystal chandelier, the Cosmopolitan's centrepiece bar soars through three separate levels. It's the middle floor where the action is, with DJ music and a buzzy crowd.

SCARPETTA

avant-garde performance-art show with which it opened, it now stages retro-style gigs, one-off events and happenings, and serves excellent cocktails and bar food.

Shows

BLUE MAN GROUP

Monte Carlo, 3770 Las Vegas Blvd S ☎702 730 7010, ⓦwww.blueman.com. Mon, Tues, Thurs, Fri & Sun 7pm & 9.30pm; Wed 7pm; Sat 4pm, 7pm & 9.30pm. $85–162. MAP P.45, POCKET MAP B2

The hilariously postmodern Blue Men are true Las Vegas favourites; kids love their craziness, adults their cleverness. Mute and lurid blue from head to toe, they combine paint-splashing, cereal-spewing clowning with pounding percussion, a relentless rock soundtrack and some amazing visual effects, to great success.

O

Bellagio, 3600 Las Vegas Blvd S ☎702 693 8866, ⓦcirquedusoleil.com. Wed–Sun 7.30pm & 10pm. $109–180. MAP P.45, POCKET MAP E7

The real star of this phenomenal show is the theatre: it centres on a metal-mesh stage, any part of which can suddenly disappear beneath the performers' feet. That makes possible a dazzling array of death-defying leaps and heart-stopping plunges that create a show you'll never forget.

ZARKANA

Aria, 3730 Las Vegas Blvd S ☎855 927 5262, ⓦ cirquedusoleil.com. Tues–Sat 7pm & 9.30pm. $69–180. MAP P.45, POCKET MAP A2

To replace its ill-fated *Viva Elvis* tribute show, Cirque du Soleil opened its first show in Las Vegas that had previously toured the world. *Zarkana* tells the story of a magician searching for his lost love and lost art, with abundant acrobatics and a rock/ electronica soundtrack.

Clubs

MARQUEE

Level 1, The Cosmopolitan, 3708 Las Vegas Blvd S ☎ 702 333 9000, ⓦ marqueelasvegas. com. Nightclub Mon, Fri & Sat 10pm–5am; Dayclub daily 10am–7pm in summer. Cover varies $20–80. MAP P.45, POCKET MAP K7

Marquee is a cutting-edge indoor-outdoor combination of a nightclub with a pool-centred "dayclub". It features a 50ft-high main floor, the Boombox, overlooking the Strip, and the Library, complete with pool tables. Add in drinks and you can expect to spend hundreds of dollars. The dayclub is smaller than at Encore (see p.82), but attracts bigger-name DJs and celebs. Buying a wristband covers the whole weekend.

ROSE.RABBIT.LIE

Level 2, The Cosmopolitan, 3708 Las Vegas Blvd S ☎ 877 667 0585, ⓦ roserabbitlie.com. Tues–Sat 5.30pm–close; cover for special events. MAP P.45, POCKET MAP J6

Self-proclaimed "modern supper club", targeted at the Cosmopolitan's hipster clientele, that remains deliberately hard to categorize. Having abandoned the

The Central Strip

Long the scene of fierce inter-casino rivalries, the central portion of the Strip now feels much more like a pedestrian neighbourhood, where visitors stroll from one casino to the next thanks to new outdoor spaces like the Linq development adjoining the Flamingo and the Roman Plaza outside Caesars Palace. What's not obvious, however, is that all those casinos, from the block-spanning behemoth Caesars Palace to grizzled veterans like the Flamingo and Harrah's across the Strip, and newcomers like Paris and Planet Hollywood to the south, now belong to the same conglomerate; you'd never guess that it's Harrah's that rules the roost.

PLANET HOLLYWOOD

3667 Las Vegas Blvd S ☎ 800 342 7724,
ⓦ www.caesars.com/planet-hollywood.
MAP P.55, POCKET MAP G9

The only Strip giant saddled with a brand name not otherwise known for gambling, **Planet Hollywood** has struggled to establish a strong identity; it's not part of the dining chain or even an independent entity. The building itself opened in 2000 as a new version of the long-established Aladdin, where Elvis Presley married Priscilla in 1966. Planet Hollywood took it over in 2004, after the Aladdin went broke in the wake of 9/11, but they in turn soon floundered and sold out to Harrah's in 2010.

Planet Hollywood has recently raised its profile by signing Britney Spears for a long-term residency. As the Aladdin, though, it always seemed to be empty, thanks to the design flaw that the door from the Strip was too hard to find – simply rectified by erecting a huge sign reading "Casino Entrance". The main attraction within is the **Miracle Mile** mall (see p.56); the actual casino is relatively small, and largely targeted, with its blaring music and flashing lights, at "hip" young visitors.

The Central Strip

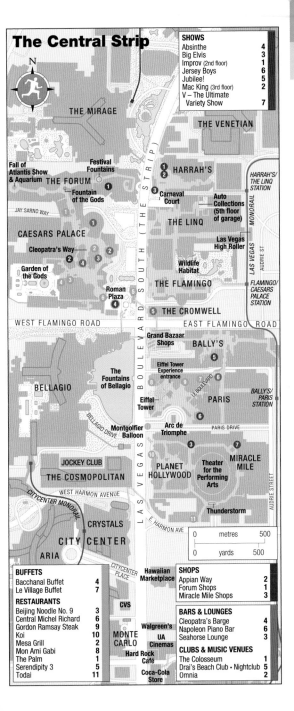

SHOWS

Absinthe	4
Big Elvis	3
Improv (2nd floor)	1
Jersey Boys	6
Jubilee!	5
Mac King (3rd floor)	2
V – The Ultimate Variety Show	7

THE MIRAGE

THE VENETIAN

Fall of Atlantis Show & Aquarium

Festival Fountains

HARRAH'S

HARRAH'S/THE LINQ STATION

THE FORUM

Fountain of the Gods

Carnaval Court

Auto Collections (5th floor of garage)

JAY SARNO WAY

THE LINQ

CAESARS PALACE

Cleopatra's Way

Las Vegas High Roller

Garden of the Gods

Wildlife Habitat

FLAMINGO/CAESARS PALACE STATION

Roman Plaza

THE FLAMINGO

THE CROMWELL

WEST FLAMINGO ROAD

EAST FLAMINGO ROAD

Grand Bazaar Shops

BALLY'S

The Fountains of Bellagio

Eiffel Tower Experience entrance

BELLAGIO

Eiffel Tower

PARIS

BALLY'S/PARIS STATION

LE BOULEVARD

Montgolfier Balloon

Arc de Triomphe

PARIS DRIVE

BELLAGIO DRIVE

JOCKEY CLUB

THE COSMOPOLITAN

WEST HARMON AVENUE

PLANET HOLLYWOOD

Theater for the Performing Arts

MIRACLE MILE

CITYCENTER MONORAIL

AUDRIE STREET

CRYSTALS

Thunderstorm

CITY CENTER

ARIA

E. HARMON AVE

| 0 | metres | 500 |
| 0 | yards | 500 |

CITYCENTER PLACE

Hawaiian Marketplace

CVS

Walgreen's

MONTE CARLO

UA Cinemas

Hard Rock Café

Coca-Cola Store

BUFFETS

Bacchanal Buffet	4
Le Village Buffet	7

RESTAURANTS

Beijing Noodle No. 9	3
Central Michel Richard	6
Gordon Ramsay Steak	9
Koi	10
Mesa Grill	2
Mon Ami Gabi	8
The Palm	1
Serendipity 3	5
Todai	11

SHOPS

Appian Way	2
Forum Shops	1
Miracle Mile Shops	3

BARS & LOUNGES

Cleopatra's Barge	4
Napoleon Piano Bar	6
Seahorse Lounge	3

CLUBS & MUSIC VENUES

The Colosseum	1
Drai's Beach Club · Nightclub	5
Omnia	2

MIRACLE MILE

Planet Hollywood, 3663 Las Vegas Blvd S
☎ 702 866 0703, ⓦ www.miraclemileshopslv
.com. MAP P.55, POCKET MAP G8

Coiled like an enormous snake around and through Planet Hollywood, the **Miracle Mile** mall is nonetheless an entirely separate operation. Built at the same time as the new Aladdin, in 2000, and still bearing traces of its original Arabian Nights theming, it was credited by some as being responsible for the Aladdin's financial failure; given the chance to stroll into a mall without having to walk through a casino en route, Strip sightseers simply ignored the Aladdin altogether. Besides a free **"thunderstorm" attraction**, the Miracle Mile holds a wide range of bars, restaurants and theatres to complement the clothing boutiques, shoe shops and galleries (see p.62).

PARIS

3655 Las Vegas Blvd S ☎ 877 796 2096,
ⓦ www.caesars.com/paris-las-vegas. MAP
P.55, POCKET MAP G8

Designed by the architects previously responsible for New York–New York, and opened a few months before the millennium, **Paris** represented the final flourish of the Las Vegas craze for building entire miniature cities. Its exterior remains one of the Strip's most enjoyable spectacles, surmounted by a gigantic Eiffel Tower whose legs crash through the ceiling into the heart of the casino itself, and anchored by the Arc de Triomphe, the Opera and a Montgolfier hot-air balloon, which becomes a glowing landmark at night.

Although it's slightly misleading to think of Paris as a separate casino at all – it was originally built as an extension to Bally's (see p.57) next door, to which it's linked by a broad corridor at the back of the building – it was an immediate hit. With both of these properties now owned by Caesars Entertainment, the tail these days is clearly wagging the dog, and Bally's feels like a minor adjunct to Paris.

Pleasing Parisian touches such as the ironwork echoing the city's Metro stations still abound throughout the interior. From the excellent **buffet** to the pastry shops and bridal wear boutiques, the great majority of Paris's shops, restaurants and bars have

PARIS

some sort of French connection. Much of it is tongue-in-cheek, so even the more tenuous links, as in calling the sports bar the **Bar du Sports**, are just part of the fun. The one area where visitors have balked at the Gallic flavour has been entertainment; Paris has long since abandoned its hopes of staging all-French productions (like, say, *Phantom of the Opera* or *Les Miserables*) in favour of safer options like Barry Manilow and Engelbert Humperdinck.

EIFFEL TOWER EXPERIENCE

Paris, 3655 Las Vegas Blvd S ☏ 888 727 4758, ⊛ www.caesars.com/paris-las-vegas. Daily 9.30am–12.30am. $14 daytime, $19 evening. MAP P.55, POCKET MAP G6

Towering 540ft over the Strip, Las Vegas's version of the **Eiffel Tower** is half the height of the Seine-side original. It's not simply a half-sized replica, however; if it was, you wouldn't be able to squeeze into the elevators, for example. In addition, this one is made of steel not iron, and doesn't have a public staircase to the top.

Visitors can either dine in the luxury restaurant 100ft up, or buy a ticket inside Paris's main entrance for the **Eiffel Tower Experience** and ride all the way to the summit viewing platform. While it offers great views all day long, the prime time to come is in the evening; as its builders always cheekily intended, the Eiffel Tower makes the perfect vantage point for watching the Bellagio fountains.

BALLY'S

3645 Las Vegas Blvd S ☏ 877 603 4390, ⊛ www.caesars.com/ballys-las-vegas. MAP P.55, POCKET MAP G7

These days, you could easily fail to notice **Bally's**, set well back from the Strip opposite

BALLY'S

Bellagio. When it opened in 1973, however, this was the MGM Grand, the biggest hotel in the world. Only after a terrible hotel fire killed 84 people here in 1980 was it bought and renamed by the gaming manufacturer Bally's, and a new MGM Grand constructed further south. Now owned by Caesars Entertainment, Bally's has become a humdrum casino that's mainly noteworthy for hosting the throwback revue show *Jubilee!* (see p.67).

Bally's was built in the era when casinos still needed huge Strip-front car parks. Legendary in Las Vegas lore as the landing site for Nicolas Cage and the parachuting Elvises in the 1992 movie *Honeymoon in Vegas*, and subsequently spanned by a network of neon-covered walkways, the former Bally's car park was due as this book went to press to become the site of an open-air "pop-up" shopping mall, the **Grand Bazaar Shops**, which may turn out to raise its profile considerably. Visit ⊛ www.grandbazaarshops.com for the latest information on the project's development.

57

CAESARS PALACE

3570 Las Vegas Blvd S ☎ 866 227 5938,
Ⓦ www.caesars.com/caesars-palace.
MAP P.55, POCKET MAP F6

Still a Las Vegas headliner in its own right, fifty years since it was built, **Caesars Palace** remains arguably the biggest name on the Strip. During the casino-building spree either side of the millennium, it slipped for a moment behind its newer rivals, to the point where Harrah's Entertainment were able to buy up control. Recognizing the prestige value of the name, however, they've not only reinvigorated Caesars and put it back on top, but changed their own name to Caesars Entertainment.

STATUE, CAESARS PALACE

Caesars Palace was originally the creation of **Jay Sarno**, a hard-gambling associate of legendary Teamsters leader Jimmy Hoffa. Cobbled together for just $24 million, it was unveiled in 1966, complete with clerks dressed as Roman centurions and cocktail waitresses kitted out like Cleopatra. Sarno himself doubled his money and sold out in 1969; he moved on to build Circus Circus, and eventually died of a heart attack in a suite at Caesars in 1984.

As well as coming up with the Caesars Palace name, designed to appeal to American and European gamblers alike, Sarno also decreed that the one thing it will never have is an apostrophe – it does not belong to Caesar, it's filled by the thousands of Caesars who choose to visit it. His crucial legacy, however, was that he'd set Caesars up on an expanse of land – originally rented from Kirk Kerkorian, who remains a major Las Vegas player to this day – that has so far proved big enough to hold every

enlargement architects have been able to imagine.

Pausing to admire Caesars Palace from the Strip is one of the great joys of visiting Las Vegas. White marble Classical statues are everywhere you look, from Julius Caesar forever hailing a cab on the main driveway to the Winged Victory of Samothrace guarding a row of gently cascading pools. Most impressive of all are the ornate fountains that surround the entrance to the Forum mall.

The central bulk of Caesars Palace is still proudly set back around 150 yards from the Strip; all that space between the casino and the Strip originally held an enormous car park. Once Las Vegas visitors began to arrive by plane not car, the gap became a deterrent to pedestrians. It was Caesars that pioneered the use of long moving walkways to haul them in – and naturally neglected to build corresponding outbound walkways to let them back out again. Bit by bit, the space has been built over. First, at the northern end, the vast **Forum** mall (see p.59) steadily extended until it reached all the way to the Strip; then the mighty **Colosseum** appeared alongside, in 2003; and more recently the **Roman Plaza** has burgeoned at the south, holding bars, restaurants and even, currently, a circus marquee, which is home to the *Absinthe* show (see p.66).

Inside, Caesars Palace bewilders most first-time visitors. Unlike newer Las Vegas properties, designed to be user-friendly and let you find what you're looking for, Caesars was laid out in the hope that gamblers might never be able to escape.

Making your way between the casino itself and the Forum is easy enough; the two simply meet on the casino floor. However, exploring the rest of Caesars Palace is less straight-forward. A network of narrow and circuitous corridors lead to the older **Appian Way** mall, which offers the chance of a close-up inspection, from directly below, of Michael-angelo's naked *David*, and Cleopatra's Way, home to the Egyptian-themed *Cleopatra's Barge* nightclub (see p.65).

Much of the rest of the property, including the luxurious **Garden of the Gods** pool complex, based on the baths of Pompeii, is only open to registered guests.

THE FORUM

3500 Las Vegas Blvd S ☎ 702 893 3807, ⓦ www.simon.com/mall. MAP P.55, POCKET MAP F5

By opening the **Forum** mall in 1992, Caesars Palace not only became the first Strip casino to turn both shopping and dining into major reasons to visit Las Vegas, it also created one of the city's most iconic attractions.

Though widely copied ever since, the Forum's domed false-sky ceiling still packs a mind-blowing punch. Designed to evoke the skyline of ancient Rome, it cycles hourly between the dazzling blue of "day" and the orange glow of "night".

Sadly, though, many of the kitschier elements of the Forum's earlier years, such as the animatronic "living statues" that adorned its centrepiece fountains, have been discarded in favour of ever more opulent and ornate decor. The most striking feature these days is the amazing convoluted spiral escalator at the Forum's main Strip entrance. Its separate moving pathways follow different trajectories, so you can never be sure they'll take you where you want to go.

The **Forum Shops** themselves still rank as Las Vegas's premier shopping spot (see p.62).

THE CROMWELL

3595 Las Vegas Blvd S ☎ 702 777 3777, Ⓦ www.caesars.com/cromwell. MAP P.55, POCKET MAP G7

Squeezed into a sandwich-sized slot at one of Las Vegas's prime intersections, the Strip's smallest casino used to be a budget alternative, known originally as the Barbary Coast and since 2007 as Bill's Gamblin' Hall & Saloon. It reopened in 2014, however, as a self-styled "boutique hotel", **The Cromwell**.

For no obvious reason, the name is intended to evoke Parisian splendour rather than those titans of English history, Thomas and Oliver. Its 188 rooms are now luxurious and expensive, while the principal new features are **Giada**, an Italian restaurant run by TV chef Giada de Laurentiis, and **Drai's** (see p.66), a massive indoor-outdoor rooftop club; the entire structure had to be strengthened to support the colossal weight of its various pools and pavilions.

THE FLAMINGO

3555 Las Vegas Blvd S ☎ 702 733 3111, Ⓦ www.caesars.com/flamingo-las-vegas. MAP P.55, POCKET MAP G6

Now that it's just another glossy casino, shoulder to shoulder in the Strip's endless procession of identikit giants, it's all but impossible to picture **the Flamingo** in its original form. Whatever anyone may tell you, when it opened in 1946 it wasn't the very first Strip resort of them all. Standing alone in the desert, however, a mile south of its nearest neighbour, the Last Frontier, the Flamingo was an enticing hundred-room oasis that put Las Vegas on the map as a glamorous, even dangerous, getaway.

Not that the Flamingo was an immediate hit. So disastrously over budget that it was forced to close within a fortnight, its initial failure cost owner Benjamin "Bugsy" Siegel his life, when his fellow mobsters gunned him down the next year. By then, however, the Flamingo was already going strong, and a wave of imitators was starting to appear.

With Bugsy a distant, sanitized memory, the Flamingo these days is much more Donny and Marie – long-term residents in its showroom – than Don Corleone. Its current owners, Caesars Entertainment, target it largely at older visitors who remember Las Vegas as it used to be back in the 1980s, when the Flamingo was still the biggest hotel in the world, and before everything had to keep reinventing itself to suit the latest trend.

From its superb neon sign and the Strip-facing patio of *Jimmy Buffet's Margaritaville* at the front, to the real-life flamingoes and penguins in the free

Wildlife Habitat and garden-set pool complex around the back, there's a lot to like about the Flamingo. As the Linq development next door expands, further upgrades and improvements will doubtless follow.

THE LINQ

3535 Las Vegas Blvd S ☎ 800 634 6441. Ⓦ www.caesars.com/linq. MAP P.55, POCKET MAP G5

Caesars Entertainment responded to MGM Resorts' construction of CityCenter by carving out its own rival "neighbourhood". Centering on the showpiece **High Roller**, it took what was previously a narrow roadway between the Flamingo and Imperial Palace casinos, and turned it into a broader pedestrian corridor of shops, bars and restaurants.

The long-standing Imperial Palace was not demolished, but totally "re-skinned", with its previous Japanese facade stripped away and its interior decor transformed. Briefly re-christened the Quad, it has now appropriated the name of the entire project – **the Linq**.

New features include a 32-lane bowling alley with its own restaurant, plus a tattoo studio, a "sneaker boutique" opened by rapper Nas, and several bars.

For the moment, one final relic of the Imperial Palace survives – the **Auto Collections**, a remarkable array of vintage cars, most of them for sale, on the fifth floor of the garage – but that will surely vanish soon.

LAS VEGAS HIGH ROLLER

3545 Las Vegas Blvd S ☎ 866 328 1888. Ⓦ www.caesars.com/linq. Daily 11.30am–2am. $25 11.30am–7pm, $35 7pm–2am. MAP P.55, POCKET MAP H6

The world's largest observation wheel, the **Las Vegas High Roller**, stands just off the Strip at the far end of the pedestrianized Linq entertainment district. At 550ft tall, it's over a hundred feet taller than the similar, 443ft London Eye, and rotates non-stop. Each of its 28 see-through cabins can carry up to forty passengers. The long-range panoramas are spectacular, though intervening buildings mean it doesn't offer ground-level views of the Strip.

HARRAH'S

3475 Las Vegas Blvd S ☎ 800 214 9110. Ⓦ www.caesars.com/harrahs-las-vegas MAP P.55, POCKET MAP G5

Harrah's is the great unsung success story of the Strip. When all its rivals were going crazy for adding eye-catching, child-friendly gimmicks, constructing replica cities and enticing young hipsters to day-night pool parties, Harrah's just carried on giving their parents the same old, same old formula of cheap eats, plentiful slots and middle-of-the-road entertainment. And it did it all so well that one by one Harrah's swallowed up all of its Central Strip rivals. Then, having bought the lot, the Harrah's organization simply changed its name to Caesars Entertainment; it's as if it never happened.

For anyone under a certain age, Harrah's itself remains as boring as ever. Walk past on the Strip, and your attention may be captured by the performers on the open-air **Carnaval Court** stage, but step inside and you're in a soporific timewarp, where country superstar Toby Keith's *I Love This Bar & Grill!* is the biggest attraction. To be fair, Harrah's does put on some good-value daytime shows, including Mac King (see p.67) and *Big Elvis* (see p.66), but it's no place for thrill-seeking sightseers.

Shops

APPIAN WAY

Caesars Palace, 3570 Las Vegas Blvd S ☎ 702 731 7222, Ⓦ www.caesars.com/caesars-palace. Store hours vary. MAP P.55, POCKET MAP F6

Much smaller than the Forum, the **Appian Way** is arrayed along two corridors just off the casino floor at Caesars Palace. Centring on an 18ft marble replica of Michaelangelo's *David*, it includes antiques and homeware store HOME, novelty gifts at PIQ, and an outlet selling Caesars' branded merchandise.

FORUM SHOPS

THE FORUM SHOPS

3500 Las Vegas Blvd S ☎ 702 893 3807, Ⓦ www.simon.com/mall. Mon–Thurs & Sun 10am–11pm, Fri & Sat 10am–midnight. MAP P.55, POCKET MAP F5

Still going strong after twenty years, the Forum Shops is foot-for-foot the country's most successful mall. That's partly because its big-name brands tend to be squeezed into smaller spaces than usual. While its two main "streets" are hardly full of surprises – expect to see an Apple Store, Gap and H&M, for example – they do offer a very intense burst of shopping.

MIRACLE MILE SHOPS

Planet Hollywood, 3663 Las Vegas Blvd S ☎ 888 800 8284, Ⓦ www.miraclemileshopslv .com. Mon–Thurs & Sun 10am–11pm, Fri & Sat 10am–midnight. MAP P.55, POCKET MAP G8

Give or take the odd fountain, the largest casino mall, the Miracle Mile Shops, could be just about anywhere. Easily entered straight from the Strip, it really is a mile long; walk from one end to the other and you'll pass a huge range of stores, from mall staples like Urban Outfitters, American Apparel, French Connection and Gap to some jaw-droppingly awful "art galleries" and a couple of ABC convenience stores.

Buffets

BACCHANAL BUFFET

Caesars Palace, 3570 Las Vegas Blvd S ☎ 702 731 7928, Ⓦ www.caesars.com /caesars-palace. Breakfast Mon–Fri 7.30–11am $29; lunch Mon–Fri 11am–3pm $36; champagne brunch Sat & Sun 8am–3pm $45; dinner Mon–Thurs & Sun 3–10pm $50, Fri & Sat 3–10pm $53. MAP P.55, POCKET MAP F6

The Strip's latest gourmet buffet – much the best at any Caesars-owned property – opened in 2012. It features five hundred freshly made items daily, from sushi, dim sum and pho soup to fresh oysters and wood-fired pizzas, prepared by chefs at nine separate "show kitchens".

LE VILLAGE BUFFET

Paris, 3655 Las Vegas Blvd S ☎ 702 946 7000, Ⓦ www.parislasvegas.com. Breakfast Mon–Fri 7–11am $22, Sat & Sun 7–10am $24; lunch Mon–Fri 11am–3pm $25; champagne brunch Sat & Sun 10am–3.30pm $31; dinner Mon–Thurs & Sun 3.30–10pm, $31, Fri & Sat 3.30–11pm, $34.. MAP P.55, POCKET MAP G7

Unique in focusing on a single cuisine – or rather, on French cuisine, from Brittany to

The Buffet of Buffets

Buffet fans should watch out for the **Buffet of Buffets pass**, sold at all the buffets in every Caesars-owned casino, which allows 24-hour unrestricted access to them all for a total cost of $55 on weekdays, $70 at weekends. Use it to eat at, say, 8pm one night, 7pm the next, and you get two dinners into the bargain. Note, however, that each visit to the Bacchanal Buffet at Caesars Palace or the Village Seafood Buffet at the Rio costs extra.

Provence – *Le Village* offers the most satisfying meal of any casino buffet. You'll find a wider array elsewhere, but if you're partial to French meat or fish, or simply fancy a fresh baguette and all the cheese you can eat, in a playful themed setting, don't miss it.

Restaurants

BEIJING NOODLE NO. 9

Caesars Palace, 3570 Las Vegas Blvd S
☎ 877 346 4642, ⓦ www.caesars.com/caesars-palace. Daily 11am–10.30pm. MAP P.55, POCKET MAP F6

Approached via aquariums that hold a thousand goldfish and resembling a pale, mysterious, underwater cavern, this Chinese noodle shop is one of Las Vegas's most enjoyable places to eat. Fortunately, the food matches the setting,

though with dim sum buns and dumplings at around $12, and the (large) noodle dishes more like $20, so too do the prices.

CENTRAL MICHEL RICHARD

Caesars Palace, 3570 Las Vegas Blvd S
☎ 702 650 5921, ⓦ centrallv.com. Daily 24hr. MAP P.55, POCKET MAP F6

Serving far better food than you'd expect from a 24-hour diner, *Central Michel Richard* consists of a spacious outdoor patio alongside Caesars' main pedestrian entrance, an indoor dining room and a walk-up bar abutting the hotel lobby. Prices and dishes on its short bistro-style menu vary slightly around the clock; standouts include the $13 matzo onion soup, covered by a deep cheesy crust, and American standards like fried or rotisserie chicken for around $26.

GORDON RAMSAY STEAK

Paris, 3655 Las Vegas Blvd S ☎ 877 346 4642, ⓦ www.caesars.com/paris-las-vegas. Daily 4.30–10.30pm. MAP P.55, POCKET MAP G7

For his first Las Vegas venture, perfectionist pottymouth Gordon Ramsay played it safe, opening a high-class steak-house near Paris's main entrance – its tunnel approach represents the trip from France to England, incidentally. Diners select from a trolley laden with marbled, aged slabs of prime meat; a superbly cooked veal chop costs $50, a strip steak $63 and the $145 tasting menu includes Beef Wellington.

costs $16 in a lunch salad, more like $30 for dinner.

MON AMI GABI

Paris, 3655 Las Vegas Blvd S ☎ 702 944 4224, ⊛ www.monamigabi.com. Mon–Fri & Sun 7am–11pm, Sat 7am–midnight. MAP P.55, POCKET MAP G7

Among the first Las Vegas restaurants to offer al fresco dining, this exuberant evocation of a Paris pavement brasserie remains the city's premier lunchtime pick. For a real taste of France, you can't beat a $14 *croque-madame* (ham, cheese and egg sandwich) for breakfast; *moules frites* (mussels and chips) for lunch ($23); or *steak frites* for dinner ($27).

THE PALM

Forum Shops, Caesars Palace ☎ 702 732 7256, ⊛ thepalm.com. Daily 11.30am–11pm. MAP P.55, POCKET MAP F5

A veteran of the Forum scene, this offshoot of the legendary New York steakhouse offers a stylish, surprisingly formal escape from the shopping mania outside. For lunch, $16 will buy you a salad, burger or sandwich. In the evening, classic Italian veal dishes cost $32–34, and a prime, 24oz rib-eye steak is $55.

SERENDIPITY 3

Caesars Palace, 3570 Las Vegas Blvd S ☎ 702 731 7373, ⊛ www.caesars.com/caesars-palace. Mon–Thurs & Sun 8am–11pm, Fri & Sat 8am–midnight. MAP P.55, POCKET MAP G6

There's nothing in the slightest bit subtle about this larger-than-life diner, set in and around a columned pavilion in Caesars' open-air Roman Plaza and open to the Strip. It simply serves unbelievably large portions of irresistibly calorific Fifties-style favourites, including burgers the size of your head and frozen hot chocolate you could swim in to cool off.

MON AMI GABI

KOI

Planet Hollywood, 3667 Las Vegas Blvd S ☎ 702 454 4555, ⊛ koirestaurant.com. Mon–Thurs & Sun 5.30–10.30pm, Fri & Sat 5.30–11.30pm. MAP P.55, POCKET MAP G8

While not the celebrity favourite it is in Hollywood, this fancy restaurant serves tasty Japanese food at what, for Las Vegas, are reasonable prices – especially considering its views of Bellagio's fountains. Sushi rolls, tuna tartare or tempura shrimp cost well under $20, mains like steamed sea bass or wasabi short ribs up to $30.

MESA GRILL

Caesars Palace, 3570 Las Vegas Blvd S ☎ 702 731 7731, ⊛ mesagrill.com. Mon–Fri 11am–2.30pm & 5–11pm, Sat & Sun 10.30am–3pm & 5–11pm. MAP P.55, POCKET MAP F6

Contemporary Southwestern chef Bobby Flay, who made his name in New York, has shown enough commitment to his Las Vegas outlet, across from the Colosseum entrance, for it to become Caesars' most dependable fine-dining restaurant. Zestful, Mexican-influenced favourites include sixteen-spice chicken, which

TODAI

Miracle Mile, Planet Hollywood, 3667 Las Vegas Blvd S ☎ 702 892 0021, ⓦ todai.com. Lunch Mon–Fri 11.30am–2.30pm $22, Sat & Sun 11.30am–2.30pm $24; dinner Mon–Thurs 5.30–9.30pm $34, Fri & Sat 5.30–10pm $36, Sun 5.30–9.30pm $36. MAP P.55, POCKET MAP G9

For fans of Japanese food, *Todai* is a dream come true – an all-you-can-eat buffet serving an almost overwhelmingly wide range of sushi and sashimi, Also on offer are all kinds of delicious noodles, soups, teriyaki meat and fried fish, plus Japanese and Western dessert options. There are reduced prices for children.

Bars and lounges

CLEOPATRA'S BARGE

Caesars Palace, 3570 Las Vegas Blvd S ☎ 702 731 7333, ⓦ www.caesars.com/caesars-palace. Daily 8.30pm–3am. MAP P.55, POCKET MAP F6

Caesars Palace was built just three years after Elizabeth Taylor's iconic performance as Cleopatra; centred on a floating replica of a Pharaonic barge, surrounded by gilded furniture and campy little nooks, this bar's been here ever since. A glorious reminder of Las Vegas's golden era, it's transformed on Friday and Saturday into the "Gossy Lounge" to stage performances by British crooner Matt Goss, of Bros fame.

NAPOLEON PIANO BAR

Paris, 3655 Las Vegas Blvd S ☎ 702 946 7000, ⓦ www.caesars.com/paris-las-vegas. Daily 4pm–1am; no cover charge. MAP P.55, POCKET MAP H7

Come in the early evening to this plush, dimly lit, bordello-red bar, poised halfway along the internal corridor that connects Paris to Bally's, and while there may be a lounge act on stage, like a vocal group or comedian, it feels like a sophisticated venue for champagne, cognac, cocktails or cigars. Between 9pm and 1am nightly, however, things turn much more raucous, as duelling pianists vie to belt out whatever the audience requests (and is prepared to tip for) – expect energetic, enthusiastic sing-along renditions of Bohemian Rhapsody and the like.

SEAHORSE LOUNGE

Caesars Palace, 3570 Las Vegas Blvd S ☎ 702 731 7778, ⓦ www.caesars.com/caesars-palace. Mon–Thurs & Sun noon–4am, Fri & Sat 24hr. MAP P.55, POCKET MAP F6

Catch your breath after walking Caesars' endless hallways in this throwback of a lounge, open to the casino floor and kitted out with plush leopardskin carpets, comfy armchairs and abundant nautical statues. The broad column at the main entrance, filled with 1700 gallons of seawater, holds live seahorses – Australian pot-bellied ones, no less.

SEAHORSE LOUNGE

Clubs and music venues

JERSEY BOYS

THE COLOSSEUM

Caesars Palace, 3570 Las Vegas Blvd S ☎ 866 227 5938, ⓦ thecolosseum.com. Showtimes and prices vary; Celine Dion typically ranges from $55–250. MAP P.55, POCKET MAP F5

Built in 2003 to house a long-term residency by Celine Dion, the 4000-seat Colosseum is the last great stronghold of the old-style Las Vegas headliner. Celine herself still returns frequently, while Elton John, Rod Stewart and Shania Twain also play regular extended engagements. Stars who appear for a night or two at a time have included Jerry Seinfeld, and even Leonard Cohen.

DRAI'S BEACHCLUB • NIGHTCLUB

The Cromwell, 3595 Las Vegas Blvd S ☎ 702 777 3800, ⓦ draislv.com. Nightclub Thurs–Sun 10pm–5am; Beachclub summer only Fri–Sun 11am–7pm. Cover $20. MAP P.55, POCKET MAP G7

This huge indoor-outdoor night-and-day club, on the roof of the Cromwell, enjoys the best Strip views imaginable. Named for EDM entrepreneur and film producer Victor Drai, previously responsible for creating XS at Encore and Tryst at Wynn Las Vegas, it programmes big-name DJs and live performers – Iggy Azalea for New Year 2014–15 – plus go-go dancers, with private poolside cabanas for high-rollers.

OMNIA

Caesars Palace, 3570 Las Vegas Blvd S ⓦ omnianightclub.com. Hours and prices to be confirmed. MAP P.55, POCKET MAP F6

Having closed its hugely popular Pure in 2014, Caesars Palace announced plans to replace it with an even more extravagant and opulent nightclub, in the same space. Part of the Hakkasan stable, Omnia was on the point of opening as this book went to press, and promised to take full advantage of the existing Strip-view rooftop garden.

Shows

ABSINTHE

Caesars Palace, 3570 Las Vegas Blvd S ☎ 800 745 3000, ⓦ absinthevegas.com. Wed–Sun 8pm & 10pm. $99–134. MAP P.55, POCKET MAP F6

Staged in the round, in a marquee on Caesars' outdoor Roman Plaza, this no-holds-barred circus-tinged burlesque show has taken Las Vegas by storm. Conceived as a crude and abrasive counterpoint to the fey whimsy of Cirque du Soleil, and eschewing PC in all its forms, it's more of a drunken night out than a traditional show, but it still charges Cirque-level prices.

BIG ELVIS

Piano Bar, Harrah's, 3475 Las Vegas Blvd S ☎ 702 369 5000, ⓦ www.caesars.com/harrahs-las-vegas. Mon, Tues, Thurs & Fri 2–6pm. Free. MAP P.55, POCKET MAP G5

Las Vegas's biggest and best-loved Elvis impersonator, Pete

Vallee, has shucked off the pounds in the last few years to become merely Large Elvis. His King-like voice still packs a powerful punch, though, and his mastery of Elvis's repertoire and easy audience rapport – requests welcome – make this the best free show in town.

IMPROV

Harrah's, 3475 Las Vegas Blvd S ☎ 702 777 7776, ⓦ www.caesars.com/harrahs-las-vegas. Tues–Thurs & Sun 8.30pm, Fri & Sat 8.30pm & 10pm. $29 or $45. MAP P.55, POCKET MAP G5

This veteran spin-off of the legendary Chicago original continues to rank as Las Vegas's best comedy club. Despite the name, bills always consist of three individual stand-ups and often feature big names trying out new material.

JERSEY BOYS

Paris, 3655 Las Vegas Blvd S ☎ 702 777 7776, ⓦ jerseyboysinfo.com/vegas. Tues 6.30pm & 9.30pm, Wed–Fri & Sun 7pm, Sat 5pm & 8.15pm. $59–245. MAP P.55, POCKET MAP G8

Broadway shows tend to come and go in Las Vegas, but *Jersey Boys*, the musical story of Frankie Valli and the Four Seasons, has run and run, first at the Palazzo and now in Paris. More than just a vehicle for some magnificent music, it's a truly engaging two-hour theatre piece, playing at an exuberant fast-talking pace that sweeps audiences along.

JUBILEE!

Bally's, 3645 Las Vegas Blvd S ☎ 800 237 7469, ⓦ www.caesars.com/ballys-las-vegas. Daily except Fri 7pm & 9.30pm (topless). $71–115. MAP P.55, POCKET MAP H7

Don't come to *Jubilee* expecting cutting-edge class. Come to enjoy the illusion that the last forty or so years never happened and that high-kicking showgirls in ostrich feathers – and, for the late shows, no bras – are still the

pinnacle of world entertainment. There's nothing else quite like it left in Vegas – don't miss it.

MAC KING

Harrah's, 3475 Las Vegas Blvd S ☎ 702 693 6143, ⓦ mackingshow.com. Tues–Sat 1pm & 3pm. $38 & $49. MAP P.55, POCKET MAP G5

Just so there's no doubt, Mac King is billed as a comedy magician. With his clownish country-boy persona, clean-talking patter, easy way with his audience and family-friendly prices – plus of course his stunning sleight of hand – he's Las Vegas's best daytime entertainment bargain.

V – THE ULTIMATE VARIETY SHOW

Miracle Mile, Planet Hollywood, 3663 Las Vegas Blvd S ☎ 702 260 7200, ⓦ vtheshow .com. Daily 7pm & 8.30pm. $70 or $90. MAP P.55, POCKET MAP H8

Rather than wide-eyed hopefuls, this enjoyable, long-running variety show features established acts happy to run through crowd-pleasing routines. Regular stars include Melinda, the "first lady of magic"; gloriously deadpan Mexican juggler Wally Eastwood; and the uproarious Russ Merlin, whose Halloween mask audience-volunteer stunt brings the house down.

JUBILEE!

The North Strip

Along the North Strip a vibrant cluster of high-end properties compete to grab visitors' attention with gimmicks like volcanoes (the Mirage), Renaissance bridges (the Venetian) and all-round gilded opulence (Wynn Las Vegas). This part of the Strip is where things turn personal, with the giant casinos owned by fiercely competitive tycoons: specifically, Sheldon Adelson, owner of the Venetian and the Palazzo, is locked in fierce rivalry with Steve Wynn, of the similarly twinned Wynn Las Vegas and Encore. Until recently, the North Strip was regarded as stretching almost all the way to downtown. Since the recession kicked in, however, almost all the veteran casinos that lay further north have either closed down or been blown up, while most of the projects scheduled to replace them have been abandoned.

THE MIRAGE

3400 Las Vegas Blvd S ☎ 702 791 7111, ⓦ mirage.com. MAP P.70, POCKET MAP F4

Unveiled as entrepreneur Steve Wynn's first Strip venture, in 1989 – when Las Vegas seemed to be in decline, and no new Strip hotels had been built for sixteen years – the **Mirage** can justly claim to have changed the city overnight. Proving that by investing in luxury, glamour and spectacle, casinos could bring back the crowds, it spawned such a host of imitators that now, ironically, it no longer stands out from the pack. Following endless mergers and buy-outs, it now belongs to MGM Resorts, which tends to concentrate its attention on its string of properties further south, while the long-departed Wynn himself has built his latest opulent resort, Wynn Las Vegas (see p.72), a short way north.

There's still plenty to like about the Mirage, from its

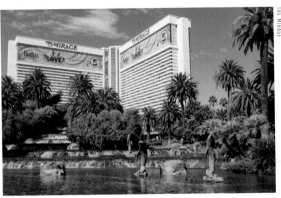

glassed-in atrium, complete with towering tropical trees, via its well-judged array of restaurants and bars, to its huge complex of pools and gardens, part of which is home to the **Secret Garden and Dolphin Habitat**. It's also still at the top of the entertainment tree, having replaced uber-camp Austrian magicians Siegfried and Roy with the Beatles showcase, *Love* (see p.84) and amazing impressionist Terry Fator (see p.85).

Steve Wynn's most radical innovation was to target the Mirage at pedestrians wandering the Strip in search of things to do. Hence the artificial **volcano** outside, which erupts at hourly intervals, on the hour, after dark.

VOLCANO, THE MIRAGE

SECRET GARDEN AND DOLPHIN HABITAT

Mirage, 3400 Las Vegas Blvd S ☎ 702 791 7188, 🌐 miragehabitat.com. Daily 10am–7pm. Adults $20, ages 4–12 $15. MAP P.70, POCKET MAP E4

Although a wayward tiger sadly curtailed the performing careers of Siegfried and Roy in 2003, the menagerie of big cats that featured in their magic is still here. Cages in the **Secret Garden and Dolphin Habitat** contain everything from black leopards and golden tigers to their signature white lions and tigers. There are also two pools of bottlenose dolphins, which interact with visitors.

TI (TREASURE ISLAND)

3300 Las Vegas Blvd S ☎ 702 894 7111, 🌐 treasureisland.com. MAP P.70, POCKET MAP G3

TI (Treasure Island) was built in 1993 as a sort of kid brother to the Mirage (see p.68) next door, with an all-pervasive pirate theme aimed at family visitors. While it's still physically connected to the Mirage by a free **monorail**, it's now under separate ownership, and distances itself from its yo-ho-ho past by using the anodyne acronym TI.

The most prominent feature of Treasure Island during its first twenty years was the shallow **lagoon** in front, home to twin replica pirate ships that were crewed first by battling buccaneers and then later by gyrating, bikini-clad "sirens" whose after-dark music-and-dance shows lured in vast crowds. Architectural theorists tied themselves in knots arguing whether Treasure Island was a building, a performance space or a theme park. Ships and sirens alike have now gone, prosaically replaced by a crass Mexican "party restaurant", *Senor Frog's*, and a huge CVS grocery/pharmacy.

Phil Ruffin, former owner of the now-vanished New Frontier, bought TI in 2008, when MGM Resorts ran short of cash to build CityCenter. He's steadily turning it into a blue-collar joint, home to nightspots like *Gilley's Saloon* (see p.81), though he's hung on to Cirque's first-ever Las Vegas show, *Mystère* (see p.84).

Chapel of the Flowers (0.5 mile) & △ A Little White Wedding Chapel (1.5 miles)

BUFFETS
The Buffet at Wynn 4
Cravings 12

RESTAURANTS
BLT Burger 14
Bouchon 11
  (in Venezia Tower,
  Level 10)
Delmonico 9
Grand Lux Café 6
Lavo 7
Pho 8
Red 8 5
Samba 13
Sinatra 2
Tao Asian Bistro 10
  (on Second Level)
Top of the World 1
  (on 106th floor)
Wazuzu 3

SHOPS
Bonanza Gifts 1
Encore Esplanade 2
Fashion Show 4
Grand Canal Shoppes 6
  (on Second Level)
Shoppes at the Palazzo 5
  (on Second Level)
Wynn Esplanade 3

BARS & LOUNGES
Gilley's Saloon 5
Japonais 10
Kahunaville 6
Parasol Up,
  Parasol Down 4
Revolution Lounge 11
V Bar 7

**CLUBS &
MUSIC VENUES**
10AK 9
Encore Beach Club 1
Tao (on Second Level) 8
Tryst 3
XS 2

SHOWS
Human Nature 3
Le Rêve 1
Love 5
Mystère 4
Terry Fator 2

Stratosphere Tower
& Thrill Rides

THE
STRATOSPHERE

Chapel of
the Bells

SLS LAS VEGAS

SLS
STATION

0 metres 500
0 yards 500

LAS VEGAS MONORAIL

WESTGATE
LAS VEGAS
STATION

WESTGATE
LAS VEGAS RESORT
(formerly
Las Vegas Hilton)

FONTAINEBLEAU
(stalled project)

(former site of)
THE RIVIERA

LAS VEGAS
CONVENTION
CENTER

CIRCUS
CIRCUS

The Adventuredome

Midway
(2nd floor)

ECHELON
(stalled
project)

Guardian
Angel
Cathedral

TRUMP
INTERNATIONAL
HOTEL

FASHION SHOW

TI
(TREASURE
ISLAND)

Grand
Canal

Volcano

THE MIRAGE

Secret Garden and
Dolphin Habitat

ENCORE

Wynn
Golf Course

Lake of
Dreams

WYNN
LAS VEGAS

THE PALAZZO

SANDS
CONVENTION
CENTER

THE VENETIAN

Madame
Tussauds

HARRAH'S

THE LINQ

HARRAH'S/THE LINQ
STATION

THE FORUM

The North Strip

THE VENETIAN

3355 Las Vegas Blvd S ☎ 702 414 1000, ⓦ www.venetian.com. MAP P.70, POCKET MAP G4

The hugely successful **Venetian** casino opened in 1999 on the site of the much-mourned Sands, the former Las Vegas home of Frank Sinatra and the Rat Pack. Even if its owner, Sheldon Adelson, may lack the design flair of Steve Wynn, he has an unarguable genius for making money. After buying the Sands in 1988, he amassed a billion-dollar fortune from the annual tech-industry trade show COMDEX and has more recently expanded his casino operations into Macau, as well as ploughing huge sums into conservative politics at home.

The Venetian itself is a re-creation of the ultimate honeymoon photo album; Adelson returned from his 1991 honeymoon trip to Venice with the idea of building a vast replica of the city. Around a dozen distinct Venetian landmarks squeeze side by side into the casino's Strip facade, while its main entrance lies between two columns, modelled on a pair brought to Venice's Piazza San Marco from Constantinople in 1172. One is topped by St Theodore, the city's original patron, the other by a winged lion representing St Mark, who became its patron in 1204.

The interior of the Venetian holds fewer specific echoes of the city. While it's the **Grand Canal** upstairs that draws in the sightseers, it's the sheer opulence elsewhere, from the huge staircases and resplendent frescoes to the endless hallways of marble tiles, which makes this the most impressive public space on the Strip. It's also among the busiest, thanks to an excellent crop of restaurants, shops and theatres, and the Sands Convention Center at the back.

When it first opened, the Venetian out-trumped Bellagio's Gallery of Fine Art (see p.49) by opening two separate Guggenheim art museums. Both have long since disappeared, but the exhibition space near the hotel lobby is still used for occasional temporary art shows.

THE GRAND CANAL

Venetian, 3355 Las Vegas Blvd S ☎ 702 414 4300, ⓦ www.venetian.com. Gondola rides indoors Mon–Thurs & Sun 10am–11pm, Fri & Sat 10am–midnight; outdoors daily 11am–10pm. $19, $76 for a 2-person private ride. MAP P.70, POCKET MAP G4 & K5

You can't have Venice without the **Grand Canal**. The Venetian has it twice – outdoors beside the Strip and as the centrepiece of its shopping and dining mall upstairs. While neither section is particularly large, let alone authentic, you have to admire the sheer nerve. With its artificial sky, the indoor segment is obviously modelled on the Forum and holds a large plaza based on St Mark's Square. Singing gondoliers take paying customers on short gondola rides along the canal.

THE GRAND CANAL

MADAME TUSSAUDS

MADAME TUSSAUDS

Venetian, 3377 Las Vegas Blvd S ☎ 866 841 3739. ⓦ www.madametussauds.com. Mon–Thurs & Sun 10am–9pm, Fri & Sat 10am–10pm. $30, ages 7–12 $20; twenty percent discount online. MAP P.78, POCKET MAP 64

Entered directly from the Strip, just off the Venetian's attractive covered Rialto Bridge, **Madame Tussauds** taps into Las Vegas's craving for close celebrity contact by allowing visitors to get personal with waxworks ranging from Brad Pitt and Daniel Craig to the bizarre body-painted Blue Men (even though they're not actually recognizable as individuals). With the single exception of Barack Obama in the White House, for whom there's an extra fee, you're free to take unlimited photos of, and with, all of your friendly, new-found waxy friends.

THE PALAZZO

3325 Las Vegas Blvd S ☎ 702 607 7777. ⓦ www.palazzo.com. MAP P.78, POCKET MAP H3

Even if owner Sheldon Adelson insists that his **Palazzo** resort is entirely separate from the Venetian next door, no one takes the distinction seriously; broad

internal walkways enable visitors to step from one property to the other and barely notice the transition. Counted as a single unit, with over seven thousand rooms, this would be the largest hotel in the world.

Considered on its own, on the other hand, the Palazzo is among the least interesting casinos in Las Vegas. As well as its own very high-end shopping mall and a decent crop of restaurants, it's home to the *Lavo* nightclub, but nothing of any interest for casual sightseers. Even the giant butterflies added to jazz up its central waterfall feature look more like one of rival Steve Wynn's cast-off ideas than anything truly original.

WYNN LAS VEGAS

3131 Las Vegas Blvd S ☎ 702 770 7000. ⓦ wynnlasvegas.com. MAP P.78, POCKET MAP J2

Steve Wynn, the man who's credited with inventing the new Las Vegas by opening first the Mirage and then Bellagio, bounced back from losing control of the Mirage organization by building his own self-named resort, **Wynn Las Vegas**, in 2005. Like his great rival at the Venetian-Palazzo next door, Sheldon Adelson, Wynn swiftly complemented Wynn Las Vegas with Encore, and now runs two nominally distinct resorts on the same site.

When Wynn bought this prime slice of real estate, it held the fabled *Desert Inn*, where Howard Hughes lived out his final years in paranoid seclusion. Steve Wynn doesn't do secondhand, though; he blew the whole place up and set to work building bigger and better than ever. The result, a majestic bronze crescent soaring skywards alongside the similar Encore, is breathtaking. Rendered almost blind by a degenerative eye disease, Wynn loves to fill his casinos with vibrant, dazzling swathes of colour – hence the plush red carpets that sweep through the interior, leading to a flower-packed **central garden** where the trees are bedecked with fairy lights and lanterns.

Because Steve Wynn wanted every Las Vegas visitor to come and admire Bellagio and the Mirage, he gave them all sorts of crowd-pleasing novelties. Wynn Las Vegas being targeted more exclusively at the luxury end of the market, with an array of consistently high-end restaurants and nightspots, holds fewer specific attractions and is therefore not quite so much of a must-see. Its most unusual feature is the **Lake of Dreams**, an expanse of water illuminated at night with changing projections, and peopled by mysterious mannequins. Unlike the Mirage's volcano, it was deliberately designed to only be visible to visitors from inside the property.

ENCORE

3121 Las Vegas Blvd S ☎ 702 770 7000, ⓦ wynnlasvegas.com. MAP P.70, POCKET MAP J1

Encore stands in the same relation to Wynn Las Vegas as does the Palazzo to the Venetian. Erected three years after its elder brother, in 2008, and joined to it seamlessly via plush corridors, it's every bit as lavish – this is where Prince Harry was photographed naked in 2012 – but offers little sense of identity in its own right. In a deliberate piece of provocative one-

upmanship, Steve Wynn built it 11ft taller than rival Sheldon Adelson's Palazzo, unveiled earlier the same year. Adelson, it's widely believed, responded by opening a large, downmarket Walgreens pharmacy at the Palazzo's Strip-level corner, thumbing his nose at the pretentious shops preferred by Wynn.

Like all Wynn's properties, Encore is ablaze with colour, like an episode of *Sesame Street* that's brought to you by the colour Red and the insects Butterfly and Dragonfly. Other than the general air of luxury, its main strategy to bring in visitors is via entertainment.

The indoor-outdoor, day-night **Encore Beach Club** (see p.82) has been a huge hit, not least with visiting British royalty, while Steve Wynn pulled off a genuine coup by luring country superstar Garth Brooks out of retirement for a long-term deal. Brooks ended his run in 2012, but Wynn has plenty more projects up his sleeve, including a showcase for songs from legendary Broadway musicals.

ENCORE

GUARDIAN ANGEL CATHEDRAL

302 Cathedral Way ☎ 702 735 5241, ⓦ dioceseoflasvegas.org. Masses Sun 8am, 9.30am, 11am, 12.30pm & 5pm. MAP P.70, POCKET MAP K1

Of all the Strip's eye-catching architectural wonders, perhaps the most unexpected stands just north of Encore – the Roman Catholic **Guardian Angel Cathedral**. It was built in 1963, on land donated by the former owner of both the Desert Inn and Stardust casinos, Moe Dalitz, a Jewish gangster from Detroit. Seeking to improve his public image, he paid modernist architect Paul Revere Williams to design this sloping tent-like structure. A stained-glass window to the right of the altar serves as a memorial to the Strip as it looked in the 1960s, depicting long-gone casinos like the Sands, the Stardust and the International.

CIRCUS CIRCUS

2880 Las Vegas Blvd S ☎ 702 734 0410, ⓦ circuscircus.com. MAP P.70, POCKET MAP K8

Guarded by the giant figure of Lucky the Clown – if you suffer from coulrophobia, or fear of clowns, you won't like Lucky one bit – the candy-striped big top of **Circus Circus** has loomed beside the Strip for half a century. In recent years, however, and despite being owned by MGM Resorts, Circus Circus has been battered and isolated by the recession. Former neighbours including the New Frontier and the Stardust have disappeared, while few of the fancy new developments that were supposed to replace them ever materialised – the Fontainebleau Las Vegas was constructed but never opened, while work on Echelon was abandoned from 2008 until 2014; Malaysian operators Genting now plan to open it as the Asian-themed Resorts World Las Vegas. Pedestrian traffic hereabouts has dwindled to nothing, to leave Circus Circus cut off from the Strip in general, and from MGM Resorts' other properties in particular.

Circus Circus has always been a strange, unsettling hybrid of circus and casino. It famously attracted the scorn of Hunter S. Thomson, who wrote in *Fear and Loathing in Las Vegas* that "Circus Circus is what the whole hep world would be doing on Saturday night if the Nazis had won the war". When it opened, in 1968, as Jay Sarno's attempt to repeat his success with Caesars Palace, it didn't include any hotel rooms and charged customers an entry fee. At first it was very much an adult playground, reflecting the sleazier side of carnival attractions. It took a few years to hit on the formula it still follows, of catering largely to families by offering **live circus acts** and other child-oriented attractions. Coupled with its low room rates, the result has been that Circus Circus has become the tackiest of the major Strip casinos.

Circus Circus is so huge that it's the only Strip casino to have an internal **monorail system**, to take guests to their rooms. With its low ceilings and endless corridors, lined with fast-food outlets and novelty stores, it's quite a maze, and it can be hard to find the mezzanine area that's home to the **Midway**. The circular stage here plays host to a constant succession of free circus acts, from trapeze artists and jugglers to tightrope walkers and, yes, clowns. Old-fashioned sideshows offer kids the chance to kick-start a lifetime's gambling habit by winning stuffed toys.

THE ADVENTUREDOME

Circus Circus, 2880 Las Vegas Blvd S ☎702 734 0410, ⓦadventuredome.com. Daily 10am–midnight during school holidays, otherwise Mon–Thurs 11am–6pm, Fri & Sat 10am–midnight, Sun 10am–9pm. $5–10 individual attractions, $30 all-day wristband, children under 4ft $17. MAP P.70, POCKET MAP J8

Las Vegas's largest theme park, the **Adventuredome**, is housed in a giant pink enclosure at the back of Circus Circus, a long walk from the Strip. Entirely indoors and on a much smaller scale than, say, Disney World or Universal Studios, it's aimed very much at children. Adults may well enjoy the twisting, looping **Canyon Blaster** and the even more ferocious, ultra-steep **El Loco**, but most of the space is given over to SpongeBob Squarepants simulator rides and the like.

SLS LAS VEGAS

2535 Las Vegas Blvd S ☎702 761 7757, ⓦslslasvegas.com. MAP P.70, POCKET MAP L2

The veteran Sahara, a Strip fixture since 1952, fell victim to the recession and closed its doors in 2011. It was not actually demolished, though, simply stripped of its former *Arabian Nights* minarets and comedy camels, and given a glossy new facade plus an injection of Philippe Starck stylings, to re-open in 2014 as **SLS Las Vegas**.

Calling itself a "boutique resort" despite having three hotel towers and over 1600 rooms, SLS is part of a rapidly expanding nightlife and hotel chain with outlets in Beverley Hills, South Beach and New York. An entertainment-based property pitched a rung or two below the Strip's top tier, it's home to an indoor-outdoor pool and nightclub, *Foxtail*, plus big-name restaurants including *Bazaar Meat* and the Starck-designed sushi place *Katsuya*.

Empty for most of the year, the vast lot across the Strip from SLS is expected to become the permanent US home of the **Rock in Rio** festival, inaugurated here in May 2015 with a line-up including Taylor Swift and Metallica.

THE ADVENTUREDOME

THE STRATOSPHERE

2000 Las Vegas Blvd S ☎800 698 6937, ⓦstratospherehotel.com. Tower Mon–Thurs & Sun 10am–1am, Fri & Sat 10am–2am. $20, discounts for guests. MAP P.70, POCKET MAP L2

At 1149ft, the **Stratosphere** makes a conveniently colossal landmark to denote the northern limit of the Strip, even if strictly speaking it's located in the city proper, a full mile north of Circus Circus, its nearest active neighbour. It took quite a feat of engineering to build the tallest structure west of the Mississippi in the shifting sands of Nevada; quite amazingly, its foundations are a mere 12ft deep.

Served by Deuce buses, but not the city's Monorail system, the Stratosphere holds nothing for sightseers apart from the **Stratosphere Tower** itself. Two observation decks, one outdoors at the very summit and the other indoors on the floor below, offer fabulous views over the city and hold fascinating displays explaining everything you can see. Most visitors are up here strictly for kicks, however, to dice with death on the array of **Thrill Rides** at the very top.

STRATOSPHERE THRILL RIDES

Stratosphere, 2000 Las Vegas Blvd S ☎702 380 7711, ⓦstratospherehotel.com. Mon–Thurs & Sun 11am–1am, Fri & Sat 11am–2am. X-Scream, Big Shot & Insanity $15 each; combination tickets up to $36 for an all-day unlimited package. SkyJump $120, minimum age 14. MAP P.70, POCKET MAP L2

The top of the Stratosphere serves as the launching point for several terrifying **thrill rides**, for daredevils only. **X-Scream** is a sort of giant boat that tips upside down a thousand feet above the Strip; **Insanity** is a crane that spins riders out over the abyss; **Big Shot** is a glorified sofa that free falls a couple of hundred feet. Worst of all is the **SkyJump**, in which harnessed jumpers step off a platform to fall 855ft.

Another one bites the dust

Yet another veteran fixture vanished from the Strip skyline in the summer of 2015, when the **Riviera** finally closed its doors after sixty years. When built in 1955, by a consortium ranging from mobsters to Marx Brothers, it was the Strip's first high-rise resort, designed to evoke the glamour of Mediterranean France; with nine storeys, it was also home to the Strip's first elevator.

During the last decade or so, as neighbours like the Stardust, the Westward Ho and Silver City were one by one blasted into oblivion, the Riviera's neon starburst facade had remained a welcome flash of colour on the North Strip. It was always a losing battle, though, and it's a sign of the times that it was ultimately purchased not by a casino operator, but by the Las Vegas Convention & Visitors Authority, which paid a reported $182.5 million to make room for a proposed expansion of the city's **Convention Center**. If all goes to plan, by the time you read this the Riviera will almost certainly have been publicly imploded.

Shops

BONANZA GIFTS

2440 Las Vegas Blvd S ☎ 702 385 7359, ⓦ www.worldslargestgiftshop.com. Daily 9am–9pm. MAP P.70, POCKET MAP L3

The self-proclaimed "World's Largest Gift Shop", where Sahara Avenue meets the Strip, is *the* place to buy Las Vegas souvenirs. Trinkets celebrating the city, old and new, include countless variations on the iconic "Welcome to Fabulous Las Vegas" sign and memorabilia from individual casinos, such as packs of used playing cards.

FASHION SHOW

3200 Las Vegas Blvd S ☎ 702 369 8382, ⓦ www.thefashionshow.com. Mon–Sat 10am–9pm, Sun 11am–7pm. MAP P.70, POCKET MAP G2

The only stand-alone shopping mall on the Strip, and for most Las Vegas visitors the only serious rival to in-casino malls such as the Forum, the Fashion Show is spread across two two-storey buildings across from Wynn Las Vegas. Despite the eye-catching circular sculpture that dangles over the pavement,

it's in no sense an attraction, simply a functional shopping destination. Unlike its Strip rivals, it's large enough to hold department stores including Macy's, Sak's Fifth Avenue, Nordstrom and Dillard's, as well as an Apple Store and the usual clothing chains.

GRAND CANAL SHOPPES

Second Level, Venetian, 3377 Las Vegas Blvd S ☎ 702 414 4500, ⓦ www .thegrandcanalshoppes.com. Mon–Thurs & Sun 10am–11pm, Fri & Sat 10am–midnight. MAP P.70, POCKET MAP K5

Arrayed along the waterfront upstairs in the Venetian, the Grand Canal Shoppes may surpass Caesars' Forum for sheer chutzpah, but as a shopping destination the mall is not a serious match. It does hold a handful of clothing chains, such as Kenneth Cole, but consists largely of souvenir and impulse-purchase stores, with a big emphasis on showy jewellery. After all, this was where Michael Jackson went on the celebrated million-dollar shopping spree that's recorded in Martin Bashir's 2003 TV documentary about the star.

SHOPPES AT THE PALAZZO

Second Level, Palazzo, 3325 Las Vegas Blvd S ☎ 702 414 4525, ⓦ www .thegrandcanalshoppes.com. Mon–Thurs & Sun 10am–11pm, Fri & Sat 10am–midnight. MAP P.70, POCKET MAP K5

More in keeping with the smart stores of Wynn Las Vegas next door than the gimmicky tone of the nearby Grand Canal, the Shoppes at the Palazzo are scattered around the resort's second floor. Few casual visitors pass this way, so the atmosphere tends to be hushed. Exclusive fashion boutiques include Jimmy Choo and Diane von Furstenberg, and there are also several expensive jewellery outlets.

FASHION SHOW

WYNN AND ENCORE ESPLANADES

Wynn Las Vegas, 3131 Las Vegas Blvd S
☎ 702 770 7000, ⓦ wynnlasvegas.com.
Mon–Thurs 10am–11pm, Fri & Sat 10am–
midnight. MAP P.70, POCKET MAP H2 & J1

There's a separate Esplanade of shops in both Wynn Las Vegas and Encore, though they're all but identical in their opulent looks and high-end prices. For ordinary mortals, fashion boutiques like Alexander McQueen and Manolo Blahnik, and the Penske-Wynn Ferrari- and Maserati-only car dealership, make for great window shopping.

Buffets

THE BUFFET AT WYNN

Wynn Las Vegas, 3131 Las Vegas Blvd S
☎ 702 770 7000, ⓦ wynnlasvegas.com.
Breakfast Mon–Fri 8am–11pm $22; brunch
Sat & Sun 8am–3pm $44; lunch Mon–Fri
11am–3pm $26; dinner Mon–Thurs & Sun
3–10pm $40, Fri & Sat 3–10.30pm $40. MAP
P.70, POCKET MAP J2

Buffets are always a high priority for Steve Wynn and at Wynn Las Vegas he's got the best buffet in town. In a plush room that oozes belle epoque excess, this is buffet food at its finest, with

dishes from lamb osso bucco and smoked duck salad to scallop ceviche and sushi rolls. While serious foodies will always prefer a real restaurant, if you've got a large appetite or are in a group with varying tastes, you won't be disappointed.

CRAVINGS

Mirage, 3400 Las Vegas Blvd S ☎ 702 792
7777, ⓦ mirage.com. Breakfast Mon–Fri
7–11am $19; brunch Mon–Fri 11am–3pm $24,
Sat & Sun 8am–3pm $34; dinner daily 3–9pm,
$30. MAP P.70, POCKET MAP F4

With its contemporary design aesthetic – rare indeed for a Las Vegas buffet, and resembling some futuristic space-age diner – *Cravings* is on a smaller scale than most of its rivals. Where possible, dishes such as stir-fries or omelettes are cooked to order; others are beautifully presented on gleaming platters. This is still mass catering – but it's a good option for a quick meal.

Restaurants

BLT BURGER

Mirage, 3400 Las Vegas Blvd S ☎ 702 792
7888, ⓦ mirage.com. Mon–Thurs & Sun
11am–2am, Fri & Sat 11am–4am. MAP P.70,
POCKET MAP F5

So-called "gourmet burger" joints are all the rage in Las Vegas. Lively long after midnight, this one, in a former tiger pen near the front of the Mirage, serves a delicious *wagyu* beef burger for $17 or a "classic" for $12, along with variations like a zesty $13 lamb tandoori burger.

BOUCHON

Level 10, Venezia Tower, Venetian, 3355
Las Vegas Blvd S ☎ 702 414 6200, ⓦ www
.thomaskeller.com. Mon–Fri 7am–1pm &
5–10pm, Sat & Sun 7am–2pm & 5–10pm. MAP
P.70, POCKET MAP H4

Thomas Keller's scrupulous evocation of a French bistro,

hidden away on the tenth floor of the Venetian's Venezia tower, may not have novelty value, but it's a lovely, relaxed spot, with plentiful outdoor seating and food that's nothing short of *magnifique*. Brunch is the best value, with sandwiches or quiche for under $20; dinner mains like *steak frites* or *sole marinière* cost $37.

BOUCHON

DELMONICO

Casino Level, Venetian, 3355 Las Vegas Blvd S ☏ 702 414 3737, ⓦ www.venetian.com. Mon–Thurs & Sun 11.30am–2pm & 5–10pm, Fri & Sat 11.30am–2pm & 5–10.30pm. MAP P.70, POCKET MAP H3

Renowned for bringing New Orleans food to the nation, chef Emeril Lagasse has made the Venetian the setting for a sophisticated steakhouse with a strong contemporary flavour. While the lunch menu centres on salads ($10) and sandwiches ($18), the big guns come out in the evening, with giant juicy steaks ($50) and starters like barbecue shrimp ($20).

GRAND LUX CAFE

Casino Level, Palazzo, 3325 Las Vegas Blvd S ☏ 702 733 7411, ⓦ www.grandluxcafe.com. Mon–Thurs & Sun 6am–2am, Fri & Sat 6am–3am. MAP P.70, POCKET MAP H3

Although it's owned by the Cheesecake Factory chain, and has itself gone national, the *Grand Lux Cafe* was originally created as a casual, but nonetheless classy, 24-hour coffee shop for the Venetian, and swiftly added this slightly smarter branch in the Palazzo. Both offer wide-ranging menus of fresh, well-prepared favourites from around the world at good prices – pizza and salad costs $12, Jamaican pork tenderloin or Yankee pot roast $19 – and have their own on-site bakeries.

LAVO

Casino Level, Palazzo, 3325 Las Vegas Blvd S ☏ 702 791 1800, ⓦ lavolv.com. Mon–Fri 5pm–midnight, Sat & Sun 10am–4pm & 5pm–midnight. MAP P.70, POCKET MAP H3

Considering it's attached to the exclusive *Lavo* nightclub, this is an oddly traditional Italian restaurant, dark and romantic rather than loud or brash. The food too is rich and authentic, and the prices relatively restrained, with pizzas for $22, pasta specials a little more and Mediterranean classics like veal *parmigiano* costing up to $46.

PHO

TI, 3300 Las Vegas Blvd S ☏ 702 894 7111, ⓦ treasureisland.com. Mon–Thurs & Sun 11am–11.30pm, Fri & Sat 11am–2.30am. MAP P.70, POCKET MAP G3

You could easily fail to notice that half the time, half of TI's 24-hour *Coffee Shop* is given over to this inexpensive and excellent Vietnamese diner. The pho of the name is steaming noodle soup; prices start at $12 and increase depending on the meat or fish you add. They also serve spring rolls and dry noodle dishes, and sneak in some sushi options and Chinese favourites too.

RED 8

Wynn Las Vegas, 3131 Las Vegas Blvd S
☎ 702 770 7000, ⓦ wynnlasvegas.com.
Mon–Thurs & Sun 11.30am–midnight, Fri &
Sat 11.30am–1am. MAP P.70, POCKET MAP J2

This decadent, deep-red,
pan-Asian restaurant makes a
stylish retreat from Wynn's
adjoining casino floor and
serves a full menu of Chinese
classics, from dim sum
dumplings at $10 to chow
mein or *ho fun* noodles for
around $20, as well as Thai
fish cakes and Malysian satay
and *laksa*.

SAMBA

Mirage, 3400 Las Vegas Blvd S ☎ 866 339
4566, ⓦ mirage.com. Daily 5–10pm. MAP P.70,
POCKET MAP F4

With its bright playful decor
and billowing couches, open
to the main walkway through
the Mirage, you can't but be
drawn towards this enticing,
high-quality Brazilian
steakhouse. Hefty meat dishes
typically cost around $30, with
starters like ceviche or
coconut prawns more like $10,
while $45 buys an all-you-
can-eat feast of barbecued
meats, from sirloin to turkey,
plus black beans and rice.

SAMBA

SINATRA

Encore, 3121 Las Vegas Blvd S ☎ 702 770
3463, ⓦ wynnlasvegas.com. Daily 5.30–10.30pm.
MAP P.70, POCKET MAP J1

The Sinatra name, licensed by
Frank's family, is of course a
gimmick, but it tells you what to
expect – the kind of idealized
Italian restaurant the Rat Pack
might have frequented back in
the 1960s, formal and romantic
and not in the slightest bit
calorie-conscious. Ol' Blue Eyes
is everywhere from the speakers
to the menu, with his favourite
spaghetti and clams for $29 and
osso bucco "My Way" for $48.

TAO ASIAN BISTRO

Second Level, Venetian, 3355 Las Vegas Blvd
S ☎ 702 388 8338, ⓦ taorestaurantlv.com.
Mon–Thurs & Sun 5pm–midnight, Fri & Sat
5pm–1am. MAP P.70, POCKET MAP J5

By far the busiest and most
profitable restaurant in the entire
USA, *Tao* is a place to come for
the experience – the over-the-
top opium-den decor, the giant
Buddha statue, the crowds of
dressed-up clubbers getting
ready to party in the *Tao*
nightclub next door – as much
as the showy Asian food. Calm
down a moment, though, and
you can enjoy a good meal
– pork or duck with sizzling
fried rice costs $15, and steak or
sea bass is around $38.

TOP OF THE WORLD

Stratosphere, 2000 Las Vegas Blvd S ☎ 702
380 7711, ⓦ topoftheworldlv.com. Lunch and
dinner Mon–Thurs & Sun 11am–10.30pm, Fri
& Sat 11am–11pm. MAP P.70, POCKET MAP L2

While it's a lot classier than the
hotel-casino far below, this
restaurant only stands out from
the pack for the compelling
reason that it's over 800ft up in
the air, and revolves every 80
minutes to give magnificent
views over the Strip. Lunchtime
is the cheapest time to come, for
a $25 sandwich or $34 steak, but

WAZUZU

dinner is much more romantic, even if the cheapest main is $40.

WAZUZU

Encore, 3121 Las Vegas Blvd S ☎ 702 770 3463, ⓦ wynnlasvegas.com. Mon–Thurs & Sun 11.30am–10.30pm, Fri & Sat 11.30am–1am. MAP P.70, POCKET MAP J1

Approached by an avenue of six colossal gilt pears, and featuring a huge crystal dragon squirming along its back wall, *Wazuzu* is by far the best-looking restaurant in Encore, and it serves the best food too. As well as sushi, it draws on Asian cuisines from Korea (short ribs $25) and Mongolia (wok-tossed-beef $21) to Thailand (chicken basil stir-fry $17). Be sure to try the *sake* too.

Bars and lounges

GILLEY'S SALOON

TI, 3300 Las Vegas Blvd S ☎ 702 894 7111, ⓦ gilleyslasvegas.com. Mon–Thurs & Sun 11am–2am, Fri & Sat 11am–4am. $10 cover for live bands. MAP P.70, POCKET MAP G3

This raucous, no-nonsense country and rodeo saloon practically defines the new TI.

Bikini-clad "Gilley Girls" ride the mechanical bulls, and you can join a free line-dancing lesson most nights at 7pm, drink two-for-one rum cocktails until 10pm, or dance to honky-tonk bands until long after midnight.

JAPONAIS

Mirage, 3400 Las Vegas Blvd S ☎ 866 339 4566, ⓦ mirage.com.. Mon–Thurs & Sun 5–10pm, Fri & Sat 5pm–midnight. MAP P.70, POCKET MAP F4

While the dining room at *Japonais*, at the heart of the Mirage, serves everything from steak to sushi, the separate lounge and bar area is a stunning, glamorous spot for pre- or after-show drinks, swathed in flowing, spotlit fabrics and offering surprisingly intimate seating areas.

KAHUNAVILLE

TI, 3300 Las Vegas Blvd S ☎ 702 894 7390, ⓦ kahunaville.com. Daily 7am–3pm. $10 cover for live bands. MAP P.70, POCKET MAP G3

Tiki-tinged and loud in looks and decibels alike, *Kahunaville* is not exactly the place for a contemplative drink. If you're looking for Las Vegas at its liveliest, however, why not kick things off with one of its super-sized frozen margaritas or "Big Kahuna" flavoured rums?

PARASOL UP, PARASOL DOWN

Wynn Las Vegas, 3131 Las Vegas Blvd S ☎ 702 770 7000, ⓦ wynnlasvegas.com. Mon–Thurs & Sun 11am–4am, Fri & Sat 11am–5am. MAP P.70, POCKET MAP J2

A quintessential example of the Wynn way with design, these twin upstairs-downstairs bars, festooned with richly coloured umbrellas and filling Wynn's central stairway, are the perfect place to admire the Lake of Dreams. A cocktail or two, and you'll feel right at Las Vegas's absurd and exhilarating heart.

REVOLUTION LOUNGE

Mirage, 3400 Las Vegas Blvd S ☎ 702 693 8300, ⓦ mirage.com. Bar daily noon–4am, free; lounge Thurs–Sun 10pm–4am, cover varies. MAP P.70, POCKET MAP F4

Indulge your inner Austin Powers with a psychedelic Sixties moment in this upbeat, flamboyant bar-lounge combo. Supposedly a joint venture between the Cirque du Soleil and the Beatles, it's split between the free-access *Abbey Road Bar*, where the wall consists of huge letters that spell out LOVE, and the *Revolution Lounge* itself, which puts on DJ sets that usually kick off with the Fab Four themselves.

V BAR

Casino Level, Venetian, 3355 Las Vegas Blvd S ☎ 702 740 6433, ⓦ vbarvegas.com. Mon–Wed & Sun 5pm–2am, Thurs–Sat 5pm–3am. Cover from $10 after 10pm. MAP P.70, POCKET MAP H4

Sophisticated lighting and decor turns this simple rectangular room near the back of the Venetian into one of the city's most elegant and sophisticated bars, filled with beautiful people both early and late, and specializing in a selection of smoky martinis and delicious rum cocktails.

Clubs and music venues

1 OAK

Mirage, 3400 Las Vegas Blvd S ☎ 702 588 5656, ⓦ 1oaklasvegas.com. Tues, Fri & Sat 10.30pm–4am. Cover varies. MAP P.70, POCKET MAP F4

An offshoot of the New York original, the Mirage's glitzy hip-hop nightclub – the name stands for "One Of A Kind" – is renowned for high-profile guest appearances, including a New Year's Eve DJ set by Kanye West. Decorated with zebra-stripe flooring and a dozen artworks by Roy Nachum, it's capable of holding well over a thousand people. Each of its two separate rooms has its own DJ booth, but most of the tables are reserved for patrons prepared to pay high prices for bottle service.

ENCORE BEACH CLUB

Encore, 3121 Las Vegas Blvd S ☎ 702 770 7300, ⓦ www.encorebeachclub.com. Late April to Oct Thurs & Sat 10am–7pm, Fri & Sun 11am–7pm. Cover $20–60. MAP P.70, POCKET MAP J1

This luxurious multilevel complex of pools, patios, bars

REVOLUTION LOUNGE

and private bungalows, in front of Encore but still thoroughly screened from the Strip, has to be the definitive expression of Las Vegas's recent craze for DJ-fuelled daytime poolside parties. No money could buy the world-wide publicity it received as the scene of Prince Harry Windsor's notorious antics in 2012, so not surprisingly it's now even more packed than ever. Exhausted revellers can escape the crowds either on pristine white "lily pads" out in the water or in private cabanas, but the pounding music will follow you everywhere. Expect to pay ultra-high prices even for regular drinks, let alone table service.

TAO

Second Level, Venetian, 3355 Las Vegas Blvd S ☎ 702 388 8338, Ⓦ taolasvegas.com. Nightclub Thurs–Sat 10pm–5am; Tao Beach late April to Oct daily 10am–sunset. Cover Thurs & Fri $20, Sat $40; weekend wristband $100. MAP P.70, POCKET MAP J5

An immediate hit in 2005 and still very much the place to be

seen, this dynamic high-concept Asian-style nightclub inevitably attracts larger crowds than its small dance floor can handle. Even on the guest list you'll have to wait to get in and you'll pay heavily for any private space. The open-air *Tao Beach* pool club is a great place to gear up for the evening. Weekend wristbands also give admission to the same owners' *Lavo* club in the adjacent Palazzo.

TRYST

Wynn Las Vegas, 3131 Las Vegas Blvd S ☎ 702 770 7300, Ⓦ www.trystlasvegas.com. Thurs–Sat 10.30pm–4am. Cover varies. MAP P.70, POCKET MAP H2

Very much in keeping with Wynn's overall decor, with its plush red sofas and drapery, the lounge areas of *Tryst* look more like an old-fashioned gentlemen's club than a twenty-first-century Las Vegas nightspot. Though it's on the small side compared with its mega-rivals and tends to attract an older, more well-heeled crowd, it also boasts a great indoor-outdoor dance floor, with an open-air terrace that faces a spectacular illuminated waterfall.

XS

Encore, 3121 Las Vegas Blvd S ☎ 702 521 4005, Ⓦ www.xslasvegas.com. Fri & Sat 9.30pm–4am, Sun & Mon 10.30pm–4am. Cover $20–30, men $50 Sat. MAP P.70, POCKET MAP J1

Where do Encore's beautiful people go after a hard day at the *Beach Club*? To the even more decadent *XS* nightclub, of course, to stay in the tropical mood, throw some moves on the massive dance-floor, drink some very classy cocktails and cool off in yet more pools.

Shows

HUMAN NATURE

Venetian, 3355 Las Vegas Blvd S ☎ 702 414 9000, ⓦ www.humannaturelive.com. Mon–Fri 7pm. $73–117. MAP P.70, POCKET MAP H4

Having enjoyed huge success with their own material back home, this wholesome Australian vocal quartet moved to Las Vegas, where their show proved enough of a smash to transfer from the (now defunct) Imperial Palace to the Venetian in 2013. Their unlikely Stateside mission, to add a down-under twist to the Motown sound, enjoys the personal blessing of Smokey Robinson himself. And no wonder – with their fabulous voices and very likeable energy, they really are superb. A smokin' live band plays the music, and the boys simply soar.

LE RÊVE

Wynn Las Vegas, 3131 Las Vegas Blvd S ☎ 702 770 9966, ⓦ wynnlasvegas.com. Mon, Tues & Fri–Sun 7pm & 9.30pm. $105–195. MAP P.70, POCKET MAP J2

Le Rêve – "The Dream" – is also the title of Steve Wynn's favourite personal Picasso and was the working name of his casino too. For the show itself,

Wynn dreamed of hiring former Cirque du Soleil talent to out-Cirque Cirque with an even more unbelievable extravaganza of colour and spectacle, featuring more water than O and wilder costumes than Mystère. In terms of sheer looks it succeeds, with astonishing coups de theatre; you'll need to overlook the vacuity of the plot, though, in which the endlessly bemused protagonist dreams of finding "the answer to life".

LOVE

Mirage, 3400 Las Vegas Blvd S ☎ 702 792 7777, ⓦ cirquedusoleil.com. Mon & Thurs–Sun 7pm & 9.30pm. $87–198. MAP P.70, POCKET MAP F5

A genuinely triumphant collaboration between Cirque du Soleil and the Beatles, in which Cirque perform superbly choreographed dancing and acrobatics to a crystal-sharp Beatles soundtrack, Love is much, much more than just another "jukebox musical". There's no story and no attempt to depict the Beatles as actual people – though eerily we hear their voices in retrieved studio chatter – just a dazzling celebration of their music and the times and places that made them who they were.

MYSTÈRE

TI, 3300 Las Vegas Blvd S ☎ 702 894 7722, ⓦ cirquedusoleil.com. Mon–Wed, Sat & Sun 7pm & 9.30pm. $69–119. MAP P.70, POCKET MAP G3

Twenty years and counting since it first opened at Treasure Island, Las Vegas's original Cirque du Soleil show is still arguably the best – you can see why it changed the Strip's entertainment scene forever, overnight. Mystère is pure

LOVE

TERRY FATOR

Fun City Motel, just north of Sahara Avenue, this little chapel conceals a romantic heart beneath its garish exterior. Draped in white silk, with the sun streaming in, it's really quite attractive – and if it was good enough for Pele, it's good enough for you. Non-denominational weddings start at $145; pay $255 or more and you get free transport to and from your hotel plus a DVD of the service.

CHAPEL OF THE FLOWERS

1717 Las Vegas Blvd S ☎ 702 735 4331, ⓦ littlechapel.com. Mon–Thurs 9am–8pm, Fri & Sat 9am–10pm. MAP P.70, POCKET MAP M1

With three separate chapels opening onto the same garden and couples queuing to take snaps at the waterfall, things can get a bit hectic at peak times, but in principle it's all surprisingly tasteful. Most popular is the Victorian chapel, with its marble floors and mahogany pews. Packages, categorized as Intimate, Elegant or Legendary, range from $495 to $9000.

spectacle, from its gorgeous costumes and billows of cascading silk to its jaw-dropping circus skills and phenomenal feats of strength.

TERRY FATOR

Mirage, 3400 Las Vegas Blvd S ☎ 702 792 7777, ⓦ mirage.com. Mon–Thurs 7.30pm. $60–150. MAP P.70, POCKET MAP F4

Yes, this middle-American ventriloquist swaps corny jokes with soft-toy puppets, but he also has an extraordinary talent: an astonishing five-octave singing voice that delivers perfect impressions of artists from Ozzy Osbourne to Etta James – all without moving his lips. Despite winning *America's Got Talent* in 2007 he is still likeable and down-to-earth.

A LITTLE WHITE WEDDING CHAPEL

1301 Las Vegas Blvd S ☎ 702 382 5943, ⓦ www.alittlewhitechapel.com. Daily 8am–midnight. MAP P.70, POCKET MAP F14

The definitive only-in-Vegas wedding chapel, as used by Joan Collins and Michael Jordan, not to mention Britney, has grown and grown to include five separate chapels. Four resemble reasonably pleasant areas in, say, a chain hotel; the fifth, the notorious "Tunnel of Love", is basically the former driveway, roofed over with angels painted on the ceiling, and hosts drive-through weddings from as little as $75 (bring your own car).

Wedding chapels

CHAPEL OF THE BELLS

2233 Las Vegas Blvd S ☎ 702 735 6803, ⓦ chapelofthebellslasvegas.com. Mon–Thurs & Sun 9am–9pm, Fri & Sat 9am–midnight. MAP P.70, POCKET MAP L3

Crammed up against the singularly unprepossessing

Downtown Las Vegas

Amounting, as far as visitors are concerned, to little more than three or four blocks, downtown is where Las Vegas started out when the railroad arrived in 1905 and also held its first casinos back in the 1930s. Many visitors prefer downtown to the Strip, feeling that by offering serious gambling, plus cheap bars, restaurants and buffets, its no-nonsense casinos represent the "real" Las Vegas. With its old-style neon signs and garish arrays of multicoloured light bulbs, it also looks much more like the Las Vegas of popular imagination than the high-tech Strip, while in the artificial sky of the Fremont Street Experience canopy it boasts a genuine must-see attraction. What's more, thanks to revitalization efforts that include the opening of the intriguing Mob Museum and the highbrow Smith Center arts centre, downtown finally appears to be on the way back up again.

FREMONT STREET EXPERIENCE

Fremont St, between Main and Fourth sts
☎ 702 678 5777, ⓦ vegasexperience.com.
Nightly, on the hour from sunset until 1am.
Free. MAP P.87, POCKET MAP G12

Wanting to give downtown a large-scale spectacle to match the Strip and make visitors feel safer outdoors at night, the downtown casinos came up with an amazing rebranding scheme – they put a roof over four city blocks and renamed downtown the **Fremont Street Experience**. After dark, the sky itself seems to become a giant movie screen – a dazzling light show of monsters and mayhem. Live bands pump out rock classics on stages set up at the main intersections – typically tribute acts to the likes of Bon Jovi or the Doors – and downtown parties until long after midnight.

Downtown Las Vegas

SLOTZILLA

Fremont St ☎702 678 5780, ⓦvegasexperience
.com. Mon–Thurs & Sun noon–midnight; Fri &
Sat noon–2am. Zipline $20, Zoomline $40.
Weight restrictions apply. MAP P.87, POCKET MAP G12

Unveiled in 2013, **SlotZilla** is
an extraordinary two-tier zip
line centring on the world's
biggest slot machine. The
120ft-tall monstrosity ejects
four riders at a time on each
level. Riders on the lower
Zipline have seats; those on
the upper Zoomline hang
prone and fly like Superman
through the canopy of the
Fremont Street Experience.

THE PLAZA

1 Main St ☎702 386 2110, ⓦwww.plazahotel
casino.com. MAP P.87, POCKET MAP F11

Once Las Vegas's railroad
station, the huge **Plaza** casino
looked set to shut shop in
2010. Surprisingly, it reopened
within a year following a $35
million face-lift. Its owners
cannily bought up the furnishings of the abandoned
Fontainebleu, and the re-
vamped Plaza now holds some
of downtown's best bars and
restaurants, including Oscar
Goodman's glass-domed
steakhouse (see p.92).

THE GOLDEN GATE

1 E Fremont St ☎702 385 1906, ⓦgolden
gatecasino.com. MAP P.87, POCKET MAP G11

Having opened in 1906, the
Golden Gate is only a year
younger than the city itself. A
railroad hotel before becoming a
casino, it still has only a hundred
rooms and remains an appealing
historic anomaly. Recent
modernizations have stripped
away some of its charms,
however, including the 99¢
shrimp cocktail bar; they're now
$2.99 from the 24-hour bakery.

GOLDEN NUGGET

129 E Fremont St ☎702 385 7111, ⓦgoldennugget.com/lasvegas. MAP P.87, POCKET MAP G12

Downtown's largest and highest-profile casino, the **Golden Nugget** has more in common with the Strip than its neighbours. Built in 1946, it's among the city's oldest casinos, but its current incarnation owes more to the 1970s, when it was acquired by a young man who was to become the leading entrepreneur of modern Las Vegas: Steve Wynn. Downtown has traditionally been characterized by hard-bitten, "sawdust joints"; Wynn gave the Golden Nugget the bright, glittery feel it retains to this day.

The most visible result of remodelling by its latest owners is the open-air swimming pool at its heart; guests who plummet down its towering waterslide pass in a clear tube through a shark-filled aquarium. Most recently, the casino opened up its Fremont Street facade, adding *Bar 46* to create a prime vantage point for the light show on Fremont Street. The casino holds little for sightseers other than an actual golden nugget; the 62-pound, million-dollar Hand of Faith was found in Australia in 1980.

BINION'S GAMBLING HALL

128 E Fremont St ☎702 382 1600, ⓦwww.binions.com. MAP P.87, POCKET MAP G12

If you think owning a casino is a sure-fire way to make money, **Binion's Gambling Hall** offers a salutary lesson. When its original owner, Benny Binion, died in 1989, this was, as Binion's Horseshoe, Las Vegas's most profitable casino. His heirs ran the place so badly that it lost its rooms and even its name. Caesars Entertainment briefly bought it to acquire the Horseshoe name and the World Series of Poker, but sold it on.

Binion's today is in a sorry state, with big empty spaces devoid even of slot machines. Its one gimmick is that visitors can pose for free photos with a million dollars in cash; it takes half an hour to get your print.

FOUR QUEENS

202 E Fremont St ☎702 385 4011, ⓦwww.fourqueens.com. MAP P.87, POCKET MAP G12

Opened in 1966 and named for its owner's four daughters, the **Four Queens** fills a whole block of Fremont Street. Its basic role is to soak up any spillover from the Golden Nugget; it holds little apart from a decent pub, the *Chicago Brewing Company* and the *Canyon Club* showroom/nightclub.

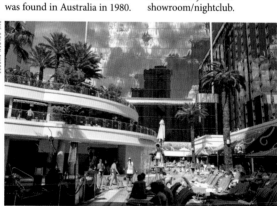

THE GOLDEN NUGGET

FREMONT HOTEL

200 E Fremont St ☎ 702 385 3232, Ⓦ www .fremontcasino.com. MAP P.87, POCKET MAP G12

Ranking a distant second behind the Golden Nugget in terms of glitz and glamour, but still ahead of its other downtown neighbours, the **Fremont Hotel** is a smart but otherwise unremarkable casino. Back in 1956 this was Nevada's tallest building; now it's noteworthy as the home of above-par restaurants, and little else.

THE D

301 E Fremont St ☎ 702 388 2400, Ⓦ www .thed.com. MAP P.87, POCKET MAP G12

A rare example of a casino completely changing both its image and its name, **The D** was until a few years ago a fake-Irish joint called Fitzgeralds, guarded by Mr O'Lucky the leprechaun. The "D" stands for downtown and Detroit, hometown of owner, Derek Stevens. He's taken advantage of the most unusual feature (that the casino boasts two storeys) to give each a different character – contemporary at street level, where go-go dancers gyrate in the "party pit", and vintage upstairs. Entertainment includes live music and comedy, plus a murder-mystery dinner theatre.

EL CORTEZ

600 E Fremont St ☎ 702 385 5200, Ⓦ el cortezhotelcasino.com. MAP P.87, POCKET MAP H12

Long celebrated as downtown's most cheerfully downmarket casino, the seventy-year-old **El Cortez** is looking remarkably spruce thanks to a freshly remodelled facade. For a taste of days gone by, as well as cheap dining and some of the best gambling odds around, it's worth braving the slightly intimidating five-minute walk east of the Fremont Street Experience even if you're not staying here.

EL CORTEZ

MAIN STREET STATION

200 N Main St ☎ 702 387 1896, Ⓦ www .mainstreetcasino.com. MAP P.87, POCKET MAP G11

At a little over twenty years old, **Main Street Station**, just north of the Plaza, is downtown's youngest casino. Despite its antique-filled Victoriana theme, it's also among the lightest and brightest casinos. While it doesn't belong to the Station chain ubiquitous elsewhere in the city, it offers a similar range of restaurants and bars.

THE NEON MUSEUM

770 Las Vegas Blvd N ☎ 702 387 6366, Ⓦ www.neonmuseum.org. Tours daily from 10am onwards; precise schedules vary. Day tours $18; after-dark tours $25. MAP P.87, POCKET MAP H10

If your appetite is whetted by the vintage signs displayed along Fremont Street, east of Las Vegas Boulevard, take a tour of the **Neon Museum** half a mile north. Treasuring signs and sculptures salvaged from long-lost casinos like the Desert Inn and the Hacienda, this is basically a junkyard, without even restrooms. Come after dark to see it at its best. The visitor centre was once the space-age lobby of *La Concha Motel*.

THE MOB MUSEUM

300 Stewart Ave ☎702 229 2734, �◍themob
museum.org. Mon–Thurs & Sun 10am–7pm,
Fri & Sat 10am–8pm. $20, ages 11–17 $14,
under-11s free. MAP P.87, POCKET MAP G11

Opened on February 14, 2012,
the 83rd anniversary of the Saint
Valentine's Day Massacre, Las
Vegas's **Mob Museum** was
designed as the lynchpin of a
campaign by then-mayor Oscar
Goodman – a former lawyer
who defended many underworld
figures – to revitalize downtown
as a tourist destination. Its full
name, the National Museum of
Organized Crime and Law
Enforcement, reflects its dual
goal of chronicling the mobsters
who once controlled the city and
the lawmen who eventually
brought them down.

The museum takes up three
storeys of the imposing former
federal courthouse, two blocks
north of Fremont Street. One
upstairs courtroom has been
restored to how it looked in
1950 when it hosted hearings by
Senator Estes' Senate committee
investigating organized crime.

With its comprehensive
displays giving the inside
stories on all sorts of Las Vegas
characters and conspiracies, the
Mob Museum is a fascinating
place to spend a few hours. It
likes to pitch itself as offering a
serious perspective on the city's
entanglement with the
underworld; however, it has a
disconcerting propensity for
trivializing and glamorizing Las
Vegas's gangster past. Lurid
panels detail, for example, the
"Mob's Greatest Hits", while
waxworks depict gory corpses.

DISCOVERY CHILDREN'S MUSEUM

360 Promenade Place ☎702 382 5437,
◍www.discoverykidslv.org. June–Sept Mon–Sat
10am–5pm, Sun noon–5pm; Oct–May Tues–Fri
9am–4pm, Sat 10am–5pm, Sun noon–5pm;
ages 1–99 $12. MAP P.87, POCKET MAP F12

Safely ensconced in spacious
new premises, next to the
Smith Center half a mile west
of Fremont Street, the long-
established **Discovery
Children's Museum** remains a
favourite with younger children
in particular. Centering on the
three-storey indoor Summit
Tower, with twelve levels of
interactive science exhibits, it
also holds play areas such as a
medieval castle.

LAS VEGAS NATURAL HISTORY MUSEUM

900 Las Vegas Blvd N ☎702 384 3466,
◍lvnhm.org. Daily 9am–4pm. $10, ages
3–11 $5. MAP P.87, POCKET MAP H10

Collections at the **Las Vegas
Natural History Museum**, a
mile north of downtown, range
from stuffed lions to animatronic dinosaurs, complemented
by tanks of live sharks and
snakes. One remarkable
specimen, a dinosaur that was
naturally mummified before it
became a fossil, prompts an
intriguing CSI-style investigation into its life and death.
There's also a replica of
Tutankhamun's tomb, donated
by the Luxor when it stripped
away its former Egyptian theme.

Shops

GAMBLERS GENERAL STORE

800 S Main St ☎ 702 382 9903, ⓦ www
.gamblersgeneralstore.com. Mon–Sat 9am–
6pm, Sun 9am–5pm. MAP P.87, POCKET MAP F13

If you love gambling, but
sometimes wish you got
something back for your
money, this is the place to
come. You can buy anything
from a $1.99 pack of playing
cards used at your favourite
casino to a $3600 roulette
wheel, strategy books and
non-gaming souvenirs.

LAS VEGAS PREMIUM OUTLETS (NORTH)

875 S Grand Central Parkway ☎ 702 474 7500,
ⓦ premiumoutlets.com. Mon–Sat 9am–9pm,
Sun 9am–8pm. MAP P.87, POCKET MAP E13

A mile west of downtown and
served by SDX buses (see
p.125) from the Strip, this huge
mall consists of over 150 stores
accessed via outdoor walkways.
Unlike the south-Strip branch
(see p.38), most are genuinely
"outlets" of well-known brands
– Diesel, Tommy Hilfiger, Nike
– so you can find real bargains.

Buffets

GOLDEN NUGGET BUFFET

Golden Nugget, 129 E Fremont St ☎ 702 385
7111, ⓦ goldennugget.com/lasvegas.
Breakfast Mon–Fri 7–10.30am $13;
champagne brunch Sat & Sun 8am–3.30pm–
$20; lunch Mon–Fri 10.30am–3.30pm $14;
dinner daily 3.30–10pm, Mon–Thurs $20, Fri–
Sun $24. MAP P.87, POCKET MAP G12

As you might expect of a casino
once owned by Steve Wynn,
the Golden Nugget boasts
downtown's best buffet, offering
a wide array of cuisines in a
humdrum space that at least
enjoys a pool view. The
weekend "seafood and more"
dinners are the best bargain.

PARADISE BUFFET AND CAFÉ

Fremont Hotel, 200 Fremont St ☎ 702 385
3232, ⓦ www.fremontcasino.com. Breakfast
Mon–Fri 7–10.30am, $7; champagne brunch
Sat & Sun 7am–3pm, $12; lunch Mon–Fri
11am–3pm, $8; dinner Mon–Thurs & Sun
4–10pm, Fri & Sat 4–11pm, Wed, Thurs,
Sat & Sun $14, Tues & Fri $20. MAP P.87,
POCKET MAP G12

Downtown has always been
popular with Hawaiian visitors,
and with palm trees and bright
colours, the Fremont's buffet
gives a taste of the islands
themselves. The food concen-
trates on American classics;
prices go up for the "seafood
bonanza" (Tues and Fri). There
is also a separate café menu.

Restaurants

HASH HOUSE A GO GO

The Plaza, 1 Main St ☎ 702 386 4646,
ⓦ hashhouseagogo.com/vegas. Mon–Thurs &
Sun 7am–11pm, Fri & Sat 7am–1am. MAP P.87,
POCKET MAP F11

This gleaming, all-day diner is
hardly the place for a romantic
rendezvous, but its "twisted farm
food" – obscenely large portions
of wholesome American country
classics like pot pie – tastes good
and is great value. It's best for
breakfast, with a varied menu.

GAMBLERS GENERAL STORE

OSCAR'S BEEF * BOOZE * BROADS

The Plaza, 1 Main St ☎702 386 7227, ⓦwww
.oscarslv.com. Mon–Thurs & Sun 5–10pm, Fri &
Sat 4.30pm–midnight. MAP P.87, POCKET MAP F11

Perched in a glass bubble
overlooking Fremont Street, this
shameless bid by former mayor
Oscar Goodman to cash in on
his larger-than-life image is a
favourite with all who remember
the old Las Vegas with affection.
Primarily a New York-style
steakhouse, serving top-quality
filet mignon or bone-in steaks
($40-plus), it also has a full
Italian-heavy menu. The
"broads" are the hostesses, who
can also be hired as dinner
companions.

SECOND STREET GRILL

Fremont Hotel, 200 E Fremont St ☎702 385
3232, ⓦwww.fremontcasino.com. Mon, Thurs
& Sun 5–10pm, Fri & Sat 5–11pm. MAP P.87,
POCKET MAP G12

Despite its dreary, windowless
setting, this gourmet restaurant
offers downtown's most inventive cuisine. Asian-influenced fish
dishes like the tuna sashimi
starter or sesame-crusted *mahi-
mahi* reflect its Hawaiian roots,
while dishes like chicken breast
with risotto and pesto are also
on offer. Mains cost $25-plus,
but the nightly special steak
dinner is just $21.

TRIPLE GEORGE GRILL

201 N Third St ☎702 384 2761,
ⓦtriplegeorgegrill.com. Mon–Fri 11am–10pm,
Sat 4–10pm. MAP P.87, POCKET MAP G11

Its speakeasy decor, mixing
exposed brickwork with wood
panelling, might not be
genuine, but this downtown
steakhouse is a real-life
hangout for local politicos and
lawyers. Come early for lunch
and watch them wheeling and
dealing in the back room over
$12 Caesar salads, $13 chicken
fettuccini or $17 steaks.

Bars and lounges

ART BAR

201 N Third St ☎702 719 5100,
ⓦdowntowngrand.com. Mon–Thurs &
Sun 3–11pm, Fri & Sat 4pm–midnight. MAP P.87,
POCKET MAP G11

Just off the lobby of the Downtown Grand – formerly the
Lady Luck – the *Art Bar* lives
up to its name by festooning
its ceiling with artworks.
Happy Hour (5–7pm) is the
ideal time to relax over a
cocktail in its plush armchairs,
perhaps after visiting the Mob
Museum opposite.

CHICAGO BREWING CO

Four Queens, 202 E Fremont St ☎702 924
5222, ⓦwww.fourqueens.com. Mon–Fri
11.30am–1.30am, Sat & Sun 10am–1.30am.
MAP P.87, POCKET MAP G12

Fremont Street's best bar and
the pick of Las Vegas's few
microbreweries is a noisy and
upbeat spot to enjoy American,
German and English-style
beers, brewed on site and sold
individually or in 64-oz, $14
"Growlers". They also serve
pizzas, wings and sandwiches.

TRIPLE GEORGE GRILL

Las Vegas acquired a performing arts centre in 2012 with the opening of this showpiece Art-Deco influenced theatre half a mile west of downtown. Its two thousand-seat auditorium hosts classical concerts, ballet and touring Broadway shows, while smaller showrooms put on a varied programme of live music and theatre.

Show

GORDIE BROWN

Golden Nugget, 129 E Fremont St ☎866 946 5336, ⓦgordiebrown.com. Tues–Thurs, Sat & Sun 7.30pm. $27.50–71.50. MAP P.87, POCKET MAP G12

High-octane impressionist Gordie Brown has an unflagging urge to please all the people, all the time. Above all he's a singer, firing off on-the-note parodies of artists from Neil Diamond to Elvis. The 50-plus demographic means some material is a bit dated, though he does cater to younger tastes with moments like the duet between Eminem and *Austin Powers'* Dr Evil.

DOWNTOWN COCKTAIL ROOM

111 Las Vegas Blvd S ☎702 880 3696, ⓦthedowntownlv.com. Mon–Fri 4pm–2am, Sat 7pm–2am. MAP P.87, POCKET MAP G12

Aimed at in-the-know locals rather than tourists, this small, dimly lit cocktail lounge, tucked away behind an industrial facade, evokes downtown's long-lost glory days. Expert mixologists create classic and original cocktails ($10–14), plus there's an early evening bar menu and live DJs after 9pm (Wed–Sat).

TRIPLE 7 RESTAURANT AND MICROBREWERY

Main Street Station, 200 N Main St ☎702 386 4442, ⓦwww.mainstreetcasino.com. Daily 11am–7am. MAP P.87, POCKET MAP G11

This cavernous pub and restaurant, at the heart of the antique-filled casino, is always full of lively, cheery drinkers savouring European brews and substantial portions of good pub grub.

Venue

SMITH CENTER FOR THE PERFORMING ARTS

361 Symphony Park Ave ☎702 749 2000, ⓦwww.thesmithcenter.com. See website for programme and prices. MAP P.87, POCKET MAP F12

Wedding chapel

GRACELAND WEDDING CHAPEL

619 S Las Vegas Blvd ☎702 382 0091, ⓦwww.gracelandchapel.com. Daily 9am–11pm. MAP P.87, POCKET MAP G13

This pretty chapel, just south of downtown, is "the home of the original Elvis wedding". You can't marry Elvis, and he's not a minister, so he can't marry you, but he can renew your vows. In the basic $199 package, the King walks you down the aisle and sings two songs; pay $799 and you get two "duelling Elvises", young and old.

The rest of the city

A glance at any map will tell you that there's a lot more to Las Vegas than simply downtown and the Strip; well over a million people live in the valley as a whole. This is not a city where under-explored neighbourhoods hold fascinating and little-known attractions, however. It's a vast and overwhelmingly residential sprawl that you'll need a car and plenty of time to explore at all thoroughly. Even then, almost all you'll find will be casinos, malls, bars and restaurants; this chapter highlights the pick of the bunch. In addition to the few that genuinely compete with the best of the Strip – the Hard Rock Hotel, the Palms and the Rio – it focuses on the so-called "locals casinos" throughout the city. While these can't match the wow factor of the Strip giants, they find their own niche by offering good-value food, drink and entertainment.

DIG THIS!

3012 S Rancho Drive ☎ 702 222 4344, ⓦ www.digthisvegas.com. Daily 8am–5pm; advance reservations essential. Big Dig $249, Mega Dig $449. MAP P.95, POCKET MAP A11.

Las Vegas has always specialized in making adult fantasies come true, but it took a truly inspired entrepreneur to come up with the idea for **Dig This!**. On a patch of desert waste ground, a mile west of the Strip, customers get to operate their very own piece of heavy machinery. On payment of a substantial fee,

anyone aged 14 and over can drive either a bulldozer or an excavator for ninety minutes; that's a Big Dig, while a Mega Dig lets you do both. Not only do you not need a driving licence, you don't even need to be old enough to have one.

After a few minutes' training you're allowed to sit alone in your vehicle, linked via headphones to an instructor who has an override switch. In a bulldozer, you pile up a huge mound of sand and then power

HARD ROCK HOTEL

Rest of the city

SHOPS	
Galleria at Sunset	3
Shepler's Western Wear	2
Zombie Apocalypse Store	1

SHOW	
Penn & Teller	1

BARS & LOUNGES	
Crown & Anchor	8
Double Down Saloon	7
Gaudi Bar	10
Ghostbar (55th floor)	4
Goodtimes Bar	9

CLUBS & MUSIC VENUES	
Flex Cocktail Lounge	1
The Joint	5
Pearl Theater	4
Piranha	6
The Railhead	2
Rain	4
VooDoo Rooftop Nightclub (51st floor)	3

BUFFETS	
Bistro Buffet	5
Carnival World	2
Feast Buffet	8
Studio B	9

RESTAURANTS	
Búzio's Seafood Restaurant	2
KJ Dim Sum	2
M&M Soul Food	1
Mr Lucky's	7
N9ne Steakhouse	5
Paymon's Mediterranean Café and Lounge	6
Ping Pang Pong	3
Roy's	4

---

the dozer over the top; in an excavator, you dig trenches and play "basketball" using your scoop. The point, of course, is that it's all fantastic fun. Whether they do it as a retirement treat or a hen party escapade, everyone who has a go seems to come away exhilarated.

GOLD COAST

4000 W Flamingo Rd 📞 702 367 7111, 🌐 www .goldcoastcasino.com. MAP P.95, POCKET MAP G15
One of Las Vegas's first "locals casinos", targeted at city residents themselves, the **Gold Coast** was erected half a mile west of the Strip in 1986. While it swiftly acquired much fancier neighbours, in the shape of the Rio and the Palms, it's hung on to its rather staid Western decor, and remains geared towards a local crowd, especially from the city's Chinatown immediately to the

north. As well as some good Asian restaurants, it also holds a seventy-lane bowling alley.

HARD ROCK HOTEL

4455 Paradise Rd 📞 702 693 5000, 🌐 www .hardrockhotel.com. MAP P.95, POCKET MAP B16
Flagged by two enormous guitars, the **Hard Rock Hotel** clamours for attention a mile east of the Strip. Best seen as a self-sufficient party resort it fills every weekend with southern Californians who come to soak up the rock'n'roll atmosphere of its clubs, music venues and "daylife"-oriented pool. For sightseers there's little here apart from endless display cabinets of stage clothes and instruments, from Elvis to Bruce and beyond. Spend a night or two, though (ideally to coincide with a big gig), and enjoy its excellent bars and restaurants, and you might just have the time of your life.

95

M RESORT

12300 Las Vegas Blvd S, Henderson ☎702 797 1000, ⓦthemresort.com. MAP P.95, POCKET MAP B14

Surveying the city from its hillside perch near the southern end of the Las Vegas Valley, ten miles south of Mandalay Bay, the shiny **M Resort** opened in 2009. Sadly, the economic climate was far from ideal for the smartest new off-Strip casino to be built in many years, so despite its impressive contemporary architecture and well considered amenities it was soon struggling. Within two years, it was snapped up by Penn Gaming for barely a quarter of its original billion-dollar cost.

Through it all, the M is looking as good as ever – almost in the Wynn class. With lavish public spaces including a lovely Palm Springs-style pool complex and great restaurants like the hugely popular *Studio B* buffet and irresistible *Baby Cakes* bakery, it's unusual in appealing to locals and visitors alike.

NATIONAL ATOMIC TESTING MUSEUM

755 E Flamingo Rd ☎702 794 5151, ⓦ.nationalatomictestingmuseum.org. Mon–Sat 10am–5pm, Sun noon–5pm. $22; senior citizens, students and ages 7–17 $20; under-6s free. MAP P.95, POCKET MAP B12

Between 1951 and 1958, a remote desert area sixty miles northwest of Las Vegas, designated as the Nevada Test Site, was used for above-ground tests of atomic bombs. Mushroom clouds were visible from the city and tourists would time their holidays so they could watch the blasts. That astonishing saga is explored in the **National Atomic Testing Museum**, which covers not only the political, scientific and

military background, but also the kitschy ways in which popular culture celebrated the bomb. A separate **Area 51** exhibit examines the even more unbelievable story of supposed "alien autopsies" in the same general vicinity.

ORLEANS

4500 W Tropicana Ave ☎702 365 7111, ⓦwww .orleanscasino.com. MAP P.95, POCKET MAP A12

Owned by the same management as the Gold Coast (see p.95), to which it's linked by free shuttles, the **Orleans** is roughly a mile due west of New York–New York. Several of its restaurants and bars play on the New Orleans connection suggested by its name, but really the emphasis is on catering to more local tastes, via such means as an eighteen-screen cinema and 24-hour bowling alley. As a place to gamble at above-average odds then relax over cheap food and entertainment, it's hard to beat.

THE PALMS

4321 W Flamingo Rd ☎702 942 7777, ⓦpalms.com. MAP P.95, POCKET MAP F16

It's a cruel drawback of running a relatively small off-Strip casino that as soon as you come up with brilliant ideas to lure visitors the big boys simply copy your innovations and entice your customers back. When it opened across from the Rio in 2001, the **Palms** became the first Las Vegas casino to tap into the twenty-first century's mix of street and celebrity culture, with an array of youth-oriented clubs and theatres that made it the hippest hangout in the city. Since then, the Strip giants have added their own state-of-the-art nightclubs and the Palms has had to keep upping its game.

Despite recent money worries, the basic elements of the Palms' winning formula remain pretty much intact. Nightlife options including the penthouse *Moon* club and the *Ghostbar* alongside it still draw in the crowds, while the Pearl Theater ranks among the city's premier concert venues. The Palms even holds a world-class recording studio as well, used by artists from Lady Gaga and Katy Perry to Usher and Tony Bennett. And with its own cinema, some decent budget restaurants and a good-value buffet, it's careful not to neglect locals either.

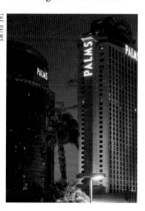

RIO

3700 W Flamingo Rd ☎ 866 746 7671, ⓦ www.caesars.com/rio-las-vegas. MAP P.95, POCKET MAP H15

A proud purple beacon, half a mile west of Caesars Palace across the interstate, when it opened in 1990, the **Rio** looked as though it might become the first casino in a generation to threaten the Strip's domination. It was independently owned and played on its Rio de Janeiro theme to build a reputation as the city's premier party scene for locals and visitors alike. Then, as now, all its guest rooms were sizeable suites, sold at highly competitive rates.

In 1999, however, the Rio was sold for almost a billion dollars to what later became Caesars Entertainment. Now run as an adjunct to its sister properties on the central Strip – to which it's linked by free shuttle buses (daily 10am–1am) from Harrah's (see p.61) and Bally's (see p.57) – it can therefore seem like something of an afterthought.

Every June and July, the Rio hosts the high-profile **World Series of Poker**; Caesars acquired the rights to the tournament when it purchased its previous home, Binion's Horseshoe, in 2004. For the rest of the year, it's best known for its sky-high *VooDoo Rooftop Nightclub* (see p.103), the Penn and Teller magic show (see p.103) and its fine selection of restaurants and buffets.

The Rio is also home to the **VooDoo Zipline** ($27.50; Mon–Thurs 11am–10pm, Fri 11am–11pm, Sat & Sun 10am–11pm), a thrill ride that connects the rooftops of its two towers, nearly 500ft above ground level. Participants are strapped into exposed side-by-side seats, and the experience resembles riding in the scariest ski lift you ever saw.

SAM'S TOWN

5111 Boulder Hwy ☎ 702 456 7777, ⓦ www
.samstownlv.com. MAP P.95, POCKET MAP D12

Best known these days as the
name of an album by Las
Vegas's favourite home-grown
band, the Killers, **Sam's Town** is
a locals casino that stands six
miles east of the Strip, alongside
the main road out to the Hoover
Dam. In the last few years, it's
updated its long-standing Wild-
West image by adding a new
affiliation with NASCAR racing,
which includes hosting the
Sam's Town 300 race every
March. It has also roofed over
its central courtyard, adding
gardens and waterfalls to create
Mystic Falls Park, the scene of
regular sound-and-light shows
(daily 2pm, 6pm, 8pm & 10pm).

SUNSET STATION

1301 W Sunset Rd, Henderson ☎ 702 547
7777, ⓦ sunsetstation.sclv.com. MAP P.95,
POCKET MAP D13

The self-styled "Spanish
Mediterranean" **Sunset Station**
casino was the first major
casino to be built in the fast-
growing suburb of Henderson,
eight miles southeast of the
Strip. It opened in 1997 as the
flagship property of the
so-called "Stations chain" of
locals casinos, and while the
chain as a whole has struggled
to stave off bankruptcy in
recent years, Sunset Station
itself is still looking good.

Its primary customers being
drawn from its own neighbourhood, Sunset Station is
crammed with community
assets like the huge 72-lane,
24-hour StrikeZone bowling
alley, a 13-screen cinema, and,
rather more questionably, the
Kids Quest daycare centre
that'll look after children while
their parents are gambling.
Some of its features would be
impressive even on the Strip,

however, including the amazing
undulating *Gaudí Bar* (see
p.102) that's the centrepiece of
the casino floor.

WESTGATE LAS VEGAS RESORT

3000 Paradise Rd ☎ 702 732 5111,
ⓦ westgateresorts.com. MAP P.95, POCKET MAP L5

The **Las Vegas Hotel** used to be
the largest and most famous
hotel in the world. Built by
legendary entrepreneur Kirk
Kerkorian in 1969, half a mile
east of the Strip, it was originally
the International Hotel.
Renamed the Las Vegas Hilton
four years later, it earned its
place in history by hosting Elvis
Presley for 837 sell-out concerts,
starting with his comeback
appearance in July 1969 and
continuing until his final Las
Vegas appearance in December
1976. A bronze statue now
commemorates the King's
achievements. Neither having its
own Monorail station nor
standing next to the city's
Convention Center spared it a
battering by the current
recession, however, and in 2012
it went into foreclosure and lost
the Hilton name. Its restaurants
and music venues are still just
about ticking along, but it feels
very peripheral indeed.

Shops

GALLERIA AT SUNSET

1300 W Sunset Rd, Henderson ☎702 434 0202, ⓦwww.galleriaatsunset.com. Mon–Sat 10am–9pm, Sun 11am–6pm. MAP P.95, POCKET MAP D13

Massive suburban shopping mall across from Sunset Station, eight miles southeast of the Strip, with five department stores and a host of middle-American chains.

SHEPLER'S WESTERN WEAR

Sam's Town, 5111 Boulder Hwy ☎702 454 5266, ⓦwww.samstownlv.com. Mon–Sat 10am–9pm, Sun 11am–9pm. MAP P.95, POCKET MAP D12

This in-casino store holds the city's finest array of Western wear. As you'd expect, there's a vast assortment of jeans and Stetsons, but the boots are the real stunners, with python- and ostrich-skin pairs from $220.

ZOMBIE APOCALYPSE STORE

3420 Spring Mountain Rd ☎702 320 0703, ⓦzombieapocalypsestore.com. Daily: summer 10am–9pm, winter 10am–7pm. MAP P.95, POCKET MAP A12

Everything you'll need to cope with the impending zombie apocalypse, from emergency rations to knives and swords. You can also sign up to spend an evening shooting "real zombies", with real paintball guns.

Buffets

BISTRO BUFFET

The Palms, 4321 W Flamingo Rd ☎702 953 7679, ⓦpalms.com. Breakfast Mon–Sat 8–11am $10; brunch Sun 8am–4pm $22; lunch Mon–Sat 11am–4pm $14; dinner daily 4–9pm $21. MAP P.95, POCKET MAP F16

A bright, modern space adjoining the main casino floor, the Palms' buffet is popular with locals for its ease of access and range of world cuisines; be sure to sample the succulent ham hocks.

CARNIVAL WORLD

Rio, 3700 W Flamingo Rd ☎702 777 7777, ⓦwww.caesars.com/rio-las-vegas. Champagne brunch Sat & Sun 8am–3pm $30; lunch Mon–Fri 11am–3pm $23; dinner daily 3–10pm $31. MAP P.95, POCKET MAP H15

Crowds flock to the Rio's all-day buffet (as opposed to its separate dinner-only *Village Seafood* buffet) to pile their plates high with almost any food they can think of, from sushi to corndogs; the choice is endless, even if the quality is predictably dependable rather than particularly delicious.

FEAST BUFFET

Sunset Station, 1301 W Sunset Rd ☎702 547 7777, ⓦsunsetstation.sclv.com. Breakfast Mon–Sat 8–11am $8; brunch Sun 8am–4pm $15; lunch Mon–Sat 11am–4pm $11; dinner daily 4–9pm $15. MAP P.95, POCKET MAP D13

Unlike their Strip rivals, all the Stations casinos still offer cut-price buffets to lure Las Vegans out to eat and gamble. Sunset Station has the nicest dining room; pick carefully and you can get a great-value meal including dishes like Indian curries, seldom seen elsewhere.

STUDIO B

M Resort, 12300 Las Vegas Blvd S ☏ 702 797 1000, ⓦ themresort.com. Lunch Mon–Fri 11am–2.30pm $16; dinner Mon–Thurs 2.30–8pm $24, Fri 2.30–8pm $40, Sat & Sun 11am–8pm $40. MAP P.95, POCKET MAP B14

Primarily this is a buffet, with food (and prices) to match the very best on the Strip, but it's also a "studio" because chefs demonstrate their art here on stage and TV screens. Prices include free wine and beer; the higher evening and weekend rates cover seafood spreads that include raw oysters. Allow time to get here – it's ten miles south of the Strip – and expect to queue to get in.

Restaurants

BÚZIO'S SEAFOOD RESTAURANT

Rio, 3700 W Flamingo Rd ☏ 702 777 7923, ⓦ www.caesars.com/rio-las-vegas. Mon–Thurs & Sun 5–10pm, Fri & Sat 5–10.30pm. MAP P.95, POCKET MAP H15

The menu at this classy dinner-only fish restaurant, looking out over the Rio's pool, draws from the best of American and Mediterranean seafood traditions, with fish stews like *bouillabaisse* and *cioppino* alongside steamed New England lobster or crab. With mains around $30 it's likely to cost $50-plus per head, but it's well worth it.

KJ DIM SUM & SEAFOOD

Rio, 3700 W Flamingo Rd ☏ 702 777 7778, ⓦ www.caesars.com/rio-las-vegas. Daily 10am–2am. MAP P.95, POCKET MAP H15

This offshoot of a popular restaurant in Las Vegas's nearby Chinatown has been an instant hit, especially for lunching locals who come to select succulent $3–6 dumplings and seafood specialities from the gleaming

dim sum trolleys. Later on, full-sized mains like sizzling scallops or whole steamed fish cost $20–30.

M&M SOUL FOOD

3923 W Charleston Blvd ☏ 702 453 7685, ⓦ mmsoulfoodcafe.com. Daily 7am–8pm. MAP P.95, POCKET MAP A11

Genuine soul food being hard to come by in Las Vegas, this neighbourhood diner is a godsend. Four miles west of downtown, it's best reached by car; you won't be in a fit state to walk anywhere once you've filled up on their succulent chicken, ribs, gumbo or cornbread.

MR LUCKY'S

Hard Rock Hotel, 4455 Paradise Rd ☏ 702 693 5592, ⓦ www.hardrockhotel.com. Daily 24hr. MAP P.95, POCKET MAP A16

A refreshing modern take on the traditional Las Vegas all-night casino coffeeshop, with an open kitchen and stylish patio seating. Whether you grab a pastrami and rye New York sandwich for lunch ($18) or stumble in for 4am spaghetti and meatballs ($14), *Mr Lucky's* offers a round-the-clock break from the Hard Rock frenzy.

N9NE STEAKHOUSE

Palms, 4321 W Flamingo Rd ☎ 702 933
9900, ⊛ www.palms.com. Mon–Thurs & Sun
5.30–10pm, Fri & Sat 5.30–11pm. MAP P.95,
POCKET MAP F16

With its waterfalls, constant
play of lights and glass-walled
celebrity areas, this glitzy,
high-concept restaurant is
very much a place to see and
be seen, but its beautifully
presented resort cuisine,
which includes sushi and
sashimi as well as steak,
cannot be faulted. You can pay
well over $50 for a steak, but
the $59 early evening prix fixe
menu (served 5–7pm) is
pretty good value.

PAYMON'S MEDITERRANEAN CAFÉ AND LOUNGE

4147 S Maryland Parkway at Flamingo Rd
☎ 702 731 6030, ⊛ paymons.com. Daily
11am–1am. MAP P.95, POCKET MAP B12

A truly local restaurant, busy
until late with students from
the nearby university. While
not exclusively vegetarian –
meat-eaters can enjoy dishes
like the $13 Persian chicken-
and-walnut *fesenjan* – it's
especially recommended for its
extensive array of Middle
Eastern classics such as falafel,
hummus and *baba ghanoush*,
available singly or in a $14
combination platter.

PING PANG PONG

Gold Coast, 4000 W Flamingo Rd ☎ 702
367 7111, ⊛ www.goldcoastcasino.com.
Daily 10am–3pm & 5pm–3am. MAP P.95,
POCKET MAP F15

You can tell straight away this
is the best Chinese restaurant
in any Las Vegas casino; most
of the diners are Chinese and
the menu is written in Chinese
characters as well as English.
Dim sum makes a lunchtime
treat, while later on you can get
chicken noodles for just $8 or
half a roast duck for $13.

ROY'S

620 E Flamingo Rd ☎ 702 691 2053,
⊛ roysrestaurant.com. Mon–Thurs
5.30–9.30pm, Fri 5.30–10pm, Sat 5–10pm,
Sun 5–9.30pm. MAP P.95, POCKET MAP B12

Generally considered the best
non-casino restaurant in Las
Vegas, Hawaiian chef Roy
Yamaguchi's dazzling,
dinner-only Pacific Rim
showcase serves exquisite
Asian-influenced cuisine.
Mains like beef short ribs or
misoyaki butterfish cost around
$30 on average, but there's also
a three-course $37 set menu.

ROY'S

Bars and lounges

CROWN & ANCHOR

1350 E Tropicana Ave ☎ 702 739 8676,
⊛ crownandanchorlv.com. Daily 24hr. MAP P.95,
POCKET MAP B12

The closest Las Vegas comes
to having a genuine British
pub – complete with Cornish
pasties, Ploughman's Lunches
and Sunday roasts – although
most of its customers, even
when it's showing European
soccer (or rather, football)
games, are students from the
nearby university.

DOUBLE DOWN SALOON

4640 Paradise Rd ☎702 791 5775, ⓦdoubledownsaloon.com. Daily 24hr. MAP P.95, POCKET MAP C17

Archetypal hole-in-the-wall dive bar, one block south of the Hard Rock, with funky murals, a hard-edged punk jukebox, no-cover live bands most nights, plus slots, blackjack and pool, and signature drinks like "ass juice" and bacon martinis.

GAUDÍ BAR

Sunset Station, 1301 W Sunset Rd, Henderson ☎702 547 7777, ⓦsunsetstation .sclv.com. Daily 24hr. MAP P.95, POCKET MAP D13

The coolest bar in any Las Vegas casino, created in honour of Catalan architect Antoni Gaudí, this bizarre fungoid excrescence undulates through the heart of Sunset Station, with cracked-up mosaics across its cave-like walls and light courtesy of the colourful stained-glass panels in the ceiling.

GHOSTBAR

Palms, 4321 W Flamingo Rd ☎702 942 6832, ⓦwww.palms.com. Daily 8pm–dawn. Cover Mon–Thurs & Sun $10, Fri & Sat $20. MAP P.95, POCKET MAP F16

What do you call a club with DJs and a cover charge but no dancing? It must be an ultra-lounge – and there's no better place to appreciate Las Vegas at night than from the deck of this 55th-floor bar, where the glass floor is replaced every two weeks.

GOODTIMES BAR

1775 E Tropicana Ave ☎702 736 9494, ⓦgoodtimeslv.com. 24hr. MAP P.95, POCKET MAP B12

This long-established and very friendly neighbourhood gay bar has increasingly established a late-night alter ago as a fully fledged club; the big night of the week is Thursday for the "Carpe Noctem" Goth extravaganza.

Clubs and music venues

FLEX COCKTAIL LOUNGE

4371 W Charleston Blvd ☎702 878 3355, ⓦflexlasvegas.com. Daily 24hr. No cover. MAP P.95, POCKET MAP A11

Lively gay bar and club, with pool tables, slots and an emphasis on upbeat action. Free entertainment nightly, including late-night drag shows Thursday and Saturday, plus half-price Happy Hours 4–7pm and 4–7am.

THE JOINT

Hard Rock Hotel, 4455 Paradise Rd ☎702 693 , ⓦwww.hardrockhotel.com. See website for schedule and prices. MAP P.95, POCKET MAP B16

Totally revamped in 2009, the Hard Rock's theatre attracts four-thousand-strong crowds to see big-name touring acts. In addition, groups like Guns'n'Roses take up residence for a month or more at a time, with typical ticket prices of around $100.

GAUDÍ BAR

THE RAILHEAD

Boulder Station, 4111 Boulder Hwy ☎ 702 547 5300, ⓦ boulderstation.sclv.com. Daily 24hr. Concert tickets typically $15–40. MAP P.95, POCKET MAP C11

A run-of-the-mill member of the Stations chain of locals casinos, Boulder Station's one bright spot is this large lounge/theatre, which hosts Latin nights on Fridays and Sundays, but also puts on solid mid-range country, soul and blues acts.

VOODOO ROOFTOP NIGHTCLUB

Rio, 3700 W Flamingo Rd ☎ 702 777 6875, ⓦ www.caesars.com/rio-las-vegas. Mon–Thurs & Sun 8pm–2am, Fri & Sat 8pm–3am. Cover $20 and up. MAP P.95, POCKET MAP J15

Long famed for its stunning 51st-floor views, this New Orleans-tinged rendezvous made its reputation as an ultra-hip drinking spot. Now a fully fledged nightclub, it's smaller than its newer rivals on the Strip, but the location is as good as ever and offers a great night out at more affordable prices.

Show

PENN & TELLER

Rio, 3700 W Flamingo Rd ☎ 702 777 2782, ⓦ pennandteller.com. Mon–Wed, Sat & Sun 9pm. $75–95. MAP P.95, POCKET MAP H15

Magicians Penn (the talkative one) and Teller (the other one) have been performing at the Rio since 2000 – while still keeping up their TV careers – but the show remains fresh, whether you simply want to swoon at the magic or you love the behind-the-scenes tricks-of-the-trade patter. They're also great with their audiences, posing and signing happily for groups of fans after the show.

PEARL THEATER

Palms, 4321 W Flamingo Rd ☎ 702 944 3200, ⓦ www.palms.com. See website for current schedule and prices. MAP P.95, POCKET MAP F16

The Palms' state-of-the-art theatre may be smaller than the Hard Rock's Joint, but with its great sound and atmosphere it attracts its fair share of major-league acts across the spectrum, from hip-hop and R&B to reggae and rock.

PIRANHA

4633 Paradise Rd ☎ 702 379 9500, ⓦ piranhavegas.com. Daily 10pm–5am. Cover varies, typically $20. MAP P.95, POCKET MAP B17

The jewel of the so-called "Fruit Loop" and the pulsating heart of Las Vegas's gay nightlife, the spectacular *Piranha* club is approached via either a fiery waterfall or a piranha-filled aquarium. The similarly lavish *8½ Ultra-lounge* alongside makes a perfect spot to kick off the night.

The deserts

Las Vegas stands close to some of the most extraordinary landscapes on the planet – the stark, sublime deserts of the American Southwest. It's possible to get a taste of this red-rock wonderland on brief forays from the city, either to Red Rock Canyon, Hoover Dam and Lake Mead, or to the Valley of Fire. To appreciate its full splendour, however, you need to venture further afield. The primary goal for many visitors is the Grand Canyon, though you'd do better visit the canyon's South Rim, almost three hundred miles east, than Grand Canyon West, which is closer to hand. Utah's Zion Canyon arguably makes an even better destination for an overnight trip from Las Vegas.

RED ROCK CANYON

17 miles west of the Strip ☎ 702 515 5367, ⓦ www.redrockcanyonlv.org. Visitor centre daily 8am–4.30pm. Scenic Drive daily: March & Oct 6am–7pm, April–Sept 6am–8pm,

Nov–Feb 6am–5pm. $7/vehicle, $3 for bikes, motorbikes and pedestrians. MAP PP.104–105.

For a quick blast of dramatic Southwestern scenery and searing desert sun, simply drive west on any road from

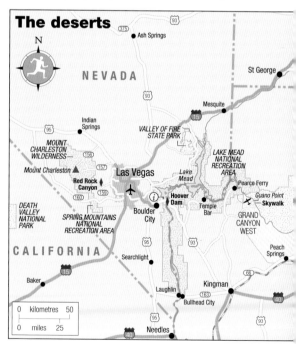

The deserts

N

NEVADA

- Ash Springs
- St George
- Mesquite
- Indian Springs
- VALLEY OF FIRE STATE PARK
- MOUNT CHARLESTON WILDERNESS
- Mount Charleston ▲
- LAKE MEAD NATIONAL RECREATION AREA
- Las Vegas
- Lake Mead
- Red Rock Canyon
- Pearce Ferry
- DEATH VALLEY NATIONAL PARK
- SPRING MOUNTAINS NATIONAL RECREATION AREA
- Boulder City
- Hoover Dam
- Temple Bar
- Guano Point
- Skywalk
- GRAND CANYON WEST

CALIFORNIA

- Searchlight
- Peach Springs
- Baker
- Kingman
- Laughlin
- Bullhead City
- Needles

0 kilometres 50
0 miles 25

the Strip. Tucked behind the first low scrubby hills, the **Red Rock Canyon National Conservation Area** centres on a desert basin at the foot of towering 3000ft cliffs. Ideally, come in the morning when the glowing red rocks are spotlit by the rising sun, and the day's heat has yet to set in

fully. Staff at the visitor centre will introduce you to this unforgiving but beautiful wilderness, as well as pointing out the hiking trails and climbing routes that set off from the one-way, thirteen-mile **Scenic Drive** just beyond, which is the only way to see the canyon itself.

HOOVER DAM

30 miles southeast of the Strip ☎702 494 2517, ⓦwww.usbr.gov/lc/hooverdam. Parking daily 8am–6.15pm; $10. Visitor Center daily: April–Sept 9am–6pm; Oct–March 9am–5pm; $10. Powerplant Tour April–Sept 9.25am–4.55pm; Oct–March 9.25am–3.55pm; $15 including Visitor Center, senior citizens & ages 4–16 $12. Dam Tour April–Sept Mon–Thurs 9.30am–4pm, Fri & Sat 9.30am–4.30pm; Oct–March daily 9.30am–3.45pm; all-inclusive fee $30, no reductions, minimum age 8. MAP PP.104–105

The mighty **Hoover Dam** straddles the Colorado River and thus the Nevada–Arizona state line as well. While this graceful 726ft-tall concrete marvel does not, as many visitors imagine, supply a significant proportion of the electricity that keeps Las Vegas running, its construction during the 1930s triggered the growth spurt, and the gambling boom, that created the modern city.

The main highway to Arizona, US-83, crosses the Colorado on a new bridge, slightly downstream from the dam. To see the dam itself, leave the highway via the spur roads at either end. For a quick look you can park briefly on the Arizona side and walk out atop the dam. Otherwise, park in the multistorey garage on the Nevada side, and walk down to the Visitor Center. Displays there explain the story and inner workings of the dam, but paying just a little extra entitles you to join a Power-plant Tour, and ride an elevator down to its base. The hour-long Dam Tour takes you right into its bowels, exploring its dank and mysterious tunnels.

LAKE MEAD

30 miles southeast of the Strip ☎702 293 8990, ⓦwww.nps.gov/lake. Visitor Center daily 9am–4.30pm. MAP PP.104–105

Created by the construction of the Hoover Dam, **Lake Mead**, east of Las Vegas, is the largest artificial lake in the USA when full. Its deep blue waters make an extraordinary contrast against the arid sands and red-rock cliffs of the desert, and attract huge numbers of visitors. Only its Nevada shoreline is accessible by road, most easily via Boulder City, a thirty-mile drive from the Strip.

Call in at the **Visitor Center** just off US-93 (closed for renovation as this book went to press, it should have reopened by the time you read this), then follow the **Lakeshore Scenic Drive** down to the lake itself. How close it approaches the shore depends on current water levels, which have remained

HOOVER DAM

low since 2002. Both **Lake Mead Marina** (☏ 702 293 3484, ⓦ www.riverlakes.com) and the neighbouring **Las Vegas Boat Harbor** (☏ 702 293 1191, ⓦ www.boatinglakemead .com) rent out boats and jet-skis, while the **Desert Princess** paddle steamer offers lake cruises from the latter ($26–61.50; ☏ 866 292 9191, ⓦ www.lakemeadcruises.com).

MOUNT CHARLESTON

A real anomaly in the Nevada deserts, and one that tends to be appreciated more by locals than by visitors, the Spring Mountain range soars into the sky forty miles northwest of the Strip. Its highest peak, **Mount Charleston**, stands just under 12,000ft tall, so its forested slopes offer a welcome escape from the summer heat of the city. Several appealing hiking trails set off across the surrounding hillsides.

To reach the mountains, head northwest out of Las Vegas on US-95 then turn west onto Hwy-157, which snakes its way into **Kyle Canyon**. Up at the head of the canyon, the **Mary Jane Falls Trail** is a 2.5-mile round-trip trek that climbs via gruelling switchbacks to a pair of waterfalls. Half a mile further on, the three-mile **Cathedral Rock Trail** involves a demanding thousand-foot ascent to a promontory with onward views to Charleston Peak itself.

That's as far as most people go, but with a little more time you can drive north from Kyle Canyon to **Lee Canyon** along Hwy-158 to enjoy far-reaching views over the desert wasteland where Nevada's notorious A-bomb tests took place in the 1950s, and then return to US-95 via Hwy-56.

VALLEY OF FIRE STATE PARK

VALLEY OF FIRE STATE PARK

Just over 50 miles northeast of the Strip ☏ 702 397 2088, ⓦ parks.nv.gov/vf.htm. Visitor centre daily 8.30am–4.30pm. $10/ vehicle. MAP PP.104–105

The most mind-blowing red-rock scenery you can see on a driving day-trip lies in the Valley of Fire State Park. To get there, follow I-15 for thirty miles towards Utah, then turn right onto Hwy-169. The park begins just after you cross the ridge of **Muddy Mountain** to look out over a magnificent sandscape of incandescent, multicoloured peaks and cliffs stretching all the way to Lake Mead.

A roadside visitor centre explains local history and geology, and displays live rattlesnakes. It marks the start of a five-mile, dead-end road that winds through amazing rock outcrops that can be explored on short hiking trails. The single most extraordinary formation, however, lies a further three miles along Hwy-169, where a natural arch – **Elephant Rock** – looks like a giant elephant poking its trunk into the sands.

Keep driving east, and you can loop back to Las Vegas along the north shore of **Lake Mead** – a total round trip of 130 miles.

Grand Canyon tours

The Grand Canyon is not as near Las Vegas as you might imagine. **Grand Canyon National Park** is two hundred miles east of Las Vegas and the **South Rim** (see p.109), which holds the park's main tourist facilities and viewpoints, is a drive of almost three hundred miles each way from the city. To see the canyon on a day-trip, there are two options: a long bus ride or an expensive flight. The majority of tours from Las Vegas therefore go to **Grand Canyon West** (see p.108), more like one hundred miles from the city, which while less spectacular is also home to the **Skywalk**, and offers the chance to land by, and even take a rafting trip on, the **Colorado River**.

With most of the operators listed below, you can choose between taking a **tour** to Grand Canyon West or the South Rim, by bus, helicopter or plane. Bus tours to Grand Canyon West typically cost around $100, or $135 including the Skywalk. The entire round-trip takes at least twelve hours, including four hours at Grand Canyon West itself. A **bus tour** to the South Rim takes over sixteen hours, with less time at the canyon itself. Prices can be as low as $80, but expect to pay more like $150 for a de luxe coach.

Flight-seeing tours to Grand Canyon West start at around $150 by plane (without landing) or $250 by helicopter. Expect to pay at least $250 by plane or $300 by helicopter for a tour that includes walking on the Skywalk, and at least $500 for a helicopter tour that lands down by the river as well.

All **flights** to the South Rim are in fixed-wing planes. A flight with a ground tour of canyon viewpoints by bus will cost around $250. Tours that include a separate helicopter flight once you arrive cost at least $400.

Note that many flights depart not from Las Vegas itself, but from **Boulder City**, thirty miles southeast. If you're hoping for an aerial view of the city into the bargain, check which airport your operator uses.

TOUR OPERATORS

Grand Canyon Airlines ☎702 835 8484, ⓦwww.grandcanyonairlines.com.
Maverick ☎702 261 0007, ⓦwww.maverickhelicopter.com.
Papillon ☎702 736 7243, ⓦwww.papillon.com.
Scenic Airlines ☎702 638 3300, ⓦwww.scenic.com.
Sundance ☎702 736 0606, ⓦwww.sundancehelicopters.com.

GRAND CANYON WEST

125 miles east of Las Vegas ⓦwww.grandcanyonwest.com. If you drive here yourself you'll still have to join a ground tour, costing a minimum of $44/person, or $88 including the Skywalk. MAP PP.104–105

The spot known as **Grand Canyon West** (or the West Rim) is not actually in Grand Canyon National Park, but on the Hualapai Indian Reservation to the west. Although it can be reached via a 125-mile one-way drive from Las Vegas, road conditions are so poor that almost all visitors fly (see box above).

At this point, close to the western end of the Grand Canyon shortly before the Colorado River spills into Lake Mead, the chasm has dwindled to around two miles wide and lacks the extraordinary sculpted rock formations you may be expecting. Instead Grand Canyon West consists of a cluster of viewpoints above drops of up to 4000ft, and looking across to similar cliffs on the far side of the river.

The major attraction is the **Skywalk**, a glass-floored, horseshoe-shaped walkway that juts out over the rim of a side canyon at Eagle Point, close to the airstrip where tours begin. The best view of the canyon itself comes from **Guano Point**, a mile or so north. The Hualapai tribe, who have lived here for over a thousand years, offer various other activities, including dance performances and barbecue cookouts.

GRAND CANYON SOUTH RIM

270 miles east of Las Vegas ☎ 928 638 7888, ⓦ www.nps.gov/grca. Entrance fee $25/ vehicle, valid for seven days. MAP PP.104–105

To see the Grand Canyon in all its glory, you have to visit **Grand Canyon National Park**. This is the area familiar from a million movies and photographs, where the canyon is studded with mighty red-rock buttes and pyramids, and measures a mile deep and eleven miles wide.

Tourist facilities, concentrated around several magnificent viewpoints along the canyon's South Rim, can be reached either by road – a total drive from Las Vegas of 270 miles, via the I-40 interstate that crosses northern Arizona fifty miles south of the canyon – or by air, to Tusayan airport, six miles south of the canyon.

While it's possible to visit the **South Rim** on a day-trip (see box opposite), it makes much more sense to drive yourself and stay at least one night. That will give you the chance to spend some time beside the canyon at sunset and dawn, and to sample the evening atmosphere of the splendid old rim-edge *El Tovar* hotel (see p.121).

ZION NATIONAL PARK

160 miles northeast of Las Vegas ☎435 772 3256, ⓦwww.nps.gov/zion. Entrance fee $25/ vehicle, valid for seven days. MAP PP.104–105

Any Las Vegas visitor hoping to see the stupendous desert scenery of the Southwest at its absolute best would do well to consider making a side trip to **Zion National Park**. Located in southwest Utah, a fast, direct drive of 160 miles northeast up I-15 from Las Vegas, it's every bit as impressive as the Grand Canyon, and offers much greater potential for an active weekend excursion from the city.

Named by nineteenth-century Mormon settlers, and carved by the Virgin River, Zion Canyon stands at the heart of the park. Unlike at the Grand Canyon, which is almost always seen from above, visitors enter by following the river upstream from the south and therefore see it from the verdant valley below. Astonishing sheer red-rock walls soar to either side, many of them topped by crests of paler sandstone that have been given fanciful names like the Court of the Patriarchs and the Great White Throne.

At the northern end of the canyon, visitors can follow the easy, mile-long **Riverside Walk** to the point where the Virgin River enters the valley. In the Zion Narrows beyond, accessible only to hardy hikers happy to wade waist-deep in ice-cold water, the towering canyon walls stand just a few feet apart. Other demanding trails switchback out of the valley to reach the desert uplands high above, and make wonderful day-hikes; the **West Rim Trail**, for example, climbs to a slender rock spur known as Angel's Landing, with a sheer quarter-of-a-mile drop to either side. Not surprisingly, Zion is also a favourite destination with rock climbers; several local operators offer guides.

Although it's possible to drive through the southern portion of the park, and continue east (towards Bryce Canyon) via an amazing 1930s tunnel, the only vehicles allowed into the narrowest part of the canyon are free shuttle buses, which depart from the visitor centre beside the park entrance.

In the canyon itself, the veteran *Zion Lodge* (see p.121) offers accommodation and dining, and the park runs large but very pleasant campgrounds. Otherwise, almost all facilities are in the gateway town of **Springdale**, in a magnificent setting just south of the park.

ZION NARROWS, ZION NATIONAL PARK

Restaurants

Mount Charleston

A CUT ABOVE

Resort on Mount Charleston, 2 Kyle Canyon Rd ☎ 702 872 5500, ⓦ mtcharlestonresort .com. Mon–Thurs & Sun 7am–9pm, Fri & Sat 7am–10pm. MAP PP.104–105

Open for all meals daily – though note the early closing time on weekdays – the light, spacious restaurant at this grand old lodge serves hearty mountain specialities such as warming buffalo and boar stew ($10), plus tasty pizzas, pasta and $25 steaks.

MOUNT CHARLESTON LODGE

5375 Kyle Canyon Rd ☎ 702 872 5408, ⓦ mtcharlestonlodge.com. Daily 8am–9pm. MAP PP.104–105

The obvious place to stop for lunch on a Mount Charleston day-trip, where the road up the mountain reaches its dead end, featuring an outdoor patio that enjoys drop-dead views. The food itself is less enthralling, with pizzas and sandwiches for around $13, burgers a little more and a three-course dinner menu for $20.

Grand Canyon

ARIZONA ROOM

Bright Angel Lodge, Grand Canyon South Rim ☎ 928 638 2631, ⓦ www.grandcanyon lodges.com. Daily: March–Oct 11.30am–3pm & 4.30–10pm; Nov & Dec 4.30–10pm. No reservations. MAP PP.104–105

This good-value restaurant, near the rim but with no views, is the most convenient place to pick up a decent meal on the South Rim. Lunchtime burgers, sandwiches and salads cost $8–12, full dinners more like $16 for chicken and $24 for steak.

EL TOVAR DINING ROOM

El Tovar, Grand Canyon South Rim ☎ 928 638 2631, ext 6432, ⓦ www.grandcanyonlodges .com. Daily 6.30am–10.45am, 11.15am–2pm & 4.30–10pm. MAP PP.104–105

The stately splendours of the timber-built *El Tovar* make an impressive setting for great food. Only the front row of tables enjoy partial views of the canyon, but this grand century-old hotel oozes old-fashioned charm and the waiters are happy to let you linger. Reserve ahead for dinner, when rich mains like half a duck or veal *jaegerschnitzel* cost $30; lunch and breakfast are first-come first-served and significantly cheaper.

Springdale

BIT & SPUR RESTAURANT

1212 Zion Park Blvd, Springdale UT ☎ 435 772 3498, ⓦ bitandspur.com. Daily 5–10pm. MAP PP.104–105

With a cosy saloon-like interior, and a terrace facing Zion's red-rock cliffs, this relaxed but high-quality Mexican/Southwestern restaurant makes a wonderful dinner spot. Chilli-rubbed steak costs $27, barbecued ribs $22 and a *chile relleno* (stuffed chilli) just $14, while the outdoor seating makes an ideal venue for a beer after a long day's hiking.

SPOTTED DOG CAFÉ

Flanigan's Inn, 428 Zion Park Blvd, Springdale UT ☎ 435 772 3244, ⓦ zion -national-park-flanigans.com. Daily 7–11am & 5–10pm. MAP PP.104–105

This very reasonably priced restaurant is attached to a motel near the Zion park entrance. In the morning it lays out a decent breakfast buffet, while the dinner menu ranges from a highly recommended $22 lamb shank to meatloaf or pasta at more like $15.

Accommodation

Choosing where to stay is the single biggest decision of any Las Vegas trip. Las Vegas is not like other destinations, where it's the city that you've come to see, and your choice of hotel makes little difference. In Las Vegas, it's the hotels that you've come to see – or rather the stupendously large casino resorts that hold not only the hotels, but also the restaurants, clubs, theatres and attractions, as well as the slot machines and gaming tables.

The fundamental choice is whether or not to stay on the **Strip**, which basically means staying in one of the colossal mega-casinos. Las Vegas is currently home to 23 of the world's 40 largest hotels, most along or very close to the Strip. Between them, they hold over 75,000 rooms, an average of almost 4000 each. All of those rooms are at least the standard of a good chain motel, invariably with en-suite bathrooms and with two queen-sized beds as the norm. Many are much more opulent; the standard rooms at places like Wynn, the Venetian and Bellagio are very plush, while every property offers **suites**.

However luxurious the rooms, the experience of staying in a hotel that has several thousand rooms has its drawbacks, including long **check-in queues** (half an hour is considered normal), a lack of personal service and endless walking to and fro. In, say, Caesars Palace or the MGM Grand, it can easily take twenty minutes to walk from your room out onto the Strip. The result is that most visitors spend their time in either their own hotel or its immediate neighbours.

The obvious alternative is to stay **downtown**, which is smaller and on a more manageable scale, with every hotel within easy walking distance from all the rest. While downtown has more affordable gambling and dining,

however, it has very few shops, shows or clubs, and lacks the jaw-dropping architecture of the Strip. It's also possible to find a room **elsewhere in the city**, either in a so-called locals casino, or in one of the many chain motels scattered around the periphery, but it's not recommended for visitors who want to experience all that makes Las Vegas unique.

As for **room rates**, it's essential to be aware that rooms change in price every night according to the level of demand. A room costing $49 on Wednesday may not still be $49 on Saturday; it might well be $199. As a rule, Friday and Saturday are the most expensive nights, though exact rates also depend on factors such as whether there's a big convention in town; a concert at a specific casino; or even a sports event elsewhere, which gamblers want to bet on in Las Vegas.

The one sure way to find a cheap rate is to visit during the week. Beyond that, it's best to book via the hotel's own website a couple of months or more in advance, or, for weekday stays only, at the very last minute. Trying to make a reservation for the coming weekend, or the weekend after, is asking for trouble.

The **prices** given here are broad guidelines to suggest what you might pay during an ordinary, quiet week, and give some idea of how hotels compare.

Resort fees and taxes

Note that in addition to the room rates shown in this chapter, guests in almost every Las Vegas hotel are also required to pay so-called resort fees, listed here separately. These additional daily fees were introduced on the pretext of covering internet access – even if you don't use it – and generally also include such things as local or even long-distance (at Wynn and Encore) phone calls, use of a fitness centre and a daily newspaper.

Hotel rates shown here do not include the additional room tax added to all bills, of twelve percent on the Strip, and thirteen percent downtown.

The Strip

ARIA > 3730 Las Vegas Blvd S ☎866 359 7757 or ☎702 590 7111, Ⓦaria.com. MAP P.45, POCKET MAP B1 If you're more of a modernist than a traditionalist – and not only appreciate Aria's sleek contemporary aesthetic, but enjoy having on-screen digital controls for everything from curtains to a/c – CityCenter's focal resort is the place for you. The rooms are classy rather than opulent, with great big beds and walk-in showers as well as tubs, but check-in tends to be slow and somewhat anarchic. **Resort fee $25/day. Mon–Thurs & Sun $169, Fri & Sat $259.**

BALLY'S > 3645 Las Vegas Blvd S ☎877 603 4390, Ⓦwww..com/ ballys-las-vegas. MAP P.57, POCKET MAP G7 Staying at Bally's is not an experience anyone gets very excited about – the rooms are spacious but otherwise run of the mill – but it is in a great location to make the most of the Strip. Above all, it's connected to its younger sister Paris next door, so guests get the benefits of staying there at much lower rates. **Resort fee $20/day. Mon–Thurs & Sun $85, Fri & Sat $169.**

BELLAGIO > 3600 Las Vegas Blvd S ☎888 987 6667 or ☎702 693 7111, Ⓦbellagio.com. MAP P.45, POCKET MAP F7 As Las Vegas is forever outdoing itself, Bellagio is no longer the cream of the crop, but by any normal standards its opulent rooms epitomize luxury, while its location and amenities can't be beaten. The premium rooms overlook the lake and its fountains, but the views from the back, over the pool, are great too. **Resort fee $25/day. Mon–Thurs & Sun $199, Fri & Sat $269.**

CAESARS PALACE > 3570 Las Vegas Blvd S ☎866 227 5938, Ⓦwww.caesars .com/caesars-palace. MAP P.57, POCKET MAP F6 Fond memories of 1960s excess will always form part of the appeal of Caesars Palace, even if these days contemporary comfort tends to win out over kitsch. The sheer scale of the place can be overwhelming, but with its top-class dining and shopping, plus a fabulous pool and spa, it still has a real cachet. For serious luxury, pay $50–100 extra to stay in the newer Augustus and Octavius towers, with separate entrances for greater privacy and convenience. **Resort fee $25/day. Mon–Thurs & Sun $229, Fri & Sat $299.**

CIRCUS CIRCUS > 2880 Las Vegas Blvd S ☎800 634 3450 or ☎702 734 0410, Ⓦcircuscircus.com. MAP P.70, POCKET MAP K8 Long a favourite with families and budget travellers, Circus Circus is showing its age; with its neighbours dropping like flies it feels like the casino time forgot. If you don't plan to linger and you have a car, its rock-bottom rates may prove irresistible. Pay a little extra to stay in its renovated towers, as opposed to the dingy Manor section. **Resort fee $13/day. Mon–Thurs & Sun $25, Fri & Sat $94.**

THE COSMOPOLITAN > 3708 Las Vegas Blvd S ☎702 698 7000, Ⓦwww .cosmopolitanlasvegas.com. MAP P.45, POCKET MAP F9 Stylish and contemporary, the Cosmopolitan makes a great option at the heart of the Strip. The guest rooms are classy and comfortable with colossal beds; even those that aren't suites have large living areas, while all except the cheapest have Strip-view balconies (a rarity in Las Vegas), and many overlook the

Bellagio fountains. There's a good spa plus top-quality restaurants and clubs, and the hotel rooms aren't far from the lobby or the parking garage. **Resort fee $25/day. Mon–Thurs & Sun $200, Fri & Sat $320.**

THE CROMWELL > 3595 Las Vegas Blvd S ☎702 777 3777, Ⓦwww .caesars.com/cromwell. MAP P.55, POCKET MAP G7 Only in Las Vegas does having 188 rooms make you a "boutique hotel"; the Strip's smallest casino reopened in 2014 as an exclusive and expensive hideaway. **Resort fee $25/day. Mon–Sun &Thurs $160, Fri & Sat $250.**

ENCORE > 3121 Las Vegas Blvd S ☎877 321 9966 or ☎702 770 8000, Ⓦwynnlasvegas.com. MAP P.70, POCKET MAP J1 Las Vegas doesn't come any more luxurious than this; Encore truly is fit for a prince (just ask Harry Windsor). The huge, high-tech rooms are more subdued and earth-toned than the lurid reds the casino might lead you to expect, and all are suites, although the beds are screened off from the living areas rather than being separate rooms. **Resort fee $25/day. Mon–Thurs & Sun $229, Fri & Sat $339.**

EXCALIBUR > 3850 Las Vegas Blvd S ☎800 879 1397 or ☎702 597 7777, Ⓦexcalibur.com. MAP P.32, POCKET MAP B4 Cross the drawbridge, enter the Disney-esque castle, wheel your bag through the casino full of kids, ride the elevator to the top of the tower and ... amazingly enough, so long as you pay a little extra for one of the renovated "wide-screen" rooms, you've found yourself a nice place to stay. The older rooms are looking very worn, though, and with its endless queues Excalibur itself can feel too big for comfort. **Resort fee $18/day. Mon–Thurs & Sun $36, Fri & Sat $120.**

THE FLAMINGO > 3555 Las Vegas Blvd S ☎888 902 9929 or ☎702 733 3111, Ⓦwww.caesars.com/flamingo-las -vegas. MAP P.55, POCKET MAP G6 So long as you stay at ground level, the Flamingo seems like a great hotel – light, airy and central, it's on a manageable scale, and has an attractive garden and pool, and even live flamingos. The rooms upstairs are very hit and miss, though, and can be grubby; only consider staying here if you find a truly exceptional rate. **Resort fee $20/day. Mon–Thurs & Sun $85, Fri & Sat $155.**

HARRAH'S > 3475 Las Vegas Blvd S ☎800 214 9110, Ⓦwww.caesars.com /harrahs-las-vegas. MAP P.55, POCKET MAP G5 There's nothing to quicken the heart about Harrah's, the middle-of-the-Strip, middle-of-the-road casino that spent a couple of decades catering so assiduously to its long-standing customers that it was able to buy all its fancier neighbours. With that kind of success, they haven't felt constrained to change much. The standard rooms are rather ordinary, though there are some fancier suites. **Resort fee $20/day. Mon–Thurs & Sun $55, Fri & Sat $130.**

THE LINQ > 3535 Las Vegas Blvd S ☎800 634 6441, Ⓦwww.caesars.com /linq. MAP P.61, POCKET MAP G5 The former Imperial Palace always ranked among the Strip's cheapest options; now re-named the Linq, it's maintaining that tradition by charging surprisingly low rates for such a central location. **Resort fee $25/day. Mon–Thurs & Sun $50, Fri & Sat $150.**

LUXOR > 3900 Las Vegas Blvd S ☎877 386 4658 or ☎702 262 4444, Ⓦluxor .com. MAP P.32, POCKET MAP B6 More than twenty years since this futuristic black-glass pyramid opened it's sadly feeling its age. It can still be a thrill to stay in one of the original rooms, with their sloping windows, but there's a reason rooms in the newer tower next door cost a little more – they're in much better condition, and also have baths and/or jacuzzis instead of showers. **Resort fee $20/day. Mon–Thurs & Sun $65, Fri & Sat $125.**

MANDALAY BAY > 3950 Las Vegas Blvd S ☎877 632 7800 or ☎702 632 7777, Ⓦmandalaybay.com. MAP P.32, POCKET MAP B7 This far south of the central Strip, it makes sense to see Mandalay Bay as a self-contained resort. If you're happy to spend long days by its extravagant pool, and while away your evenings in its fine restaurants, bars, clubs and theatres, then it's well worth considering. The rooms are very comfortable, with both baths and walk-in showers. **Resort fee $25/day. Mon–Thurs & Sun $90, Fri & Sat $150.**

MGM GRAND > 3799 Las Vegas Blvd S 📞877 880 0880 or 📞702 891 7777, 🌐mgmgrand.com. MAP P.32, POCKET MAP C3 While it may not be the world's largest hotel any more, the MGM Grand feels too big for its own good; once you've queued to check in and walked half a mile to your room, you may not feel up to venturing out to explore. Accommodation has been largely upgraded at the expense of its former character; the dark brown palette could be any convention hotel, anywhere. **Resort fee $25/day. Mon–Thurs & Sun $95, Fri & Sat $165.**

THE MIRAGE > 3400 Las Vegas Blvd S 📞800 374 9000 or 📞702 791 7111, 🌐mirage.com. MAP P.70, POCKET MAP F4 The casino that gave Vegas a new definition of luxury seems like a fairly modest choice almost thirty years on, in that its rooms are smaller than the norm, and its bathrooms even smaller. They're still more than comfortable, though, with Strip and volcano views, and in a good location with excellent on-site amenities. **Resort fee $25/day. Mon–Thurs & Sun $125, Fri & Sat $240.**

MONTE CARLO > 3770 Las Vegas Blvd S 📞888 529 4828 or 📞702 730 7777, 🌐montecarlo.com. MAP P.45, POCKET MAP C2 Anywhere else, the three thousand-room Monte Carlo might seem like a big deal. In Las Vegas, it's barely visible, serving simply as an access route to CityCenter. Don't expect remarkable rooms, but in their anonymous way they're spruce and smart, and with the top-notch pool it's well worth considering if you can find a decent rate. **Resort fee $20/day. Mon–Thurs & Sun $66, Fri & Sat $135.**

NEW YORK–NEW YORK > 3790 Las Vegas Blvd S 📞866 815 4365 or 📞702 740 6969, 🌐newyork newyork.com. MAP P.32, POCKET MAP C3 Spending a night or two in Las Vegas's own Big Apple makes a more appealing prospect than a stay at most of its larger, less compact neighbours. Whether you opt for a "Park Avenue" or a slightly larger "Madison Avenue" room, the guest rooms are attractive and readily accessible, with some nice Art Deco touches, and the casino itself holds some excellent bars and restaurants. **Resort fee $20/day. Mon–Thurs & Sun $85, Fri & Sat $160.**

THE PALAZZO > 3325 Las Vegas Blvd S 📞866 263 3001 or 📞702 607 7777, 🌐www.palazzo.com. MAP P.70, POCKET MAP H3 Staying at the Palazzo

Las Vegas's most luxurious spas

State-of-the-art spas in Las Vegas's top casinos pamper visitors with pools, steam rooms, fitness facilities and massage services. Daily entry normally costs around $30, and massages and other treatments from around $100 per half hour. Often, during busy periods, only guests staying in the relevant casino can use its spa. The following are the very best:

Aria	The Spa	Daily 5.30am–8pm	📞702 590 9600
Bellagio	Spa Bellagio	Daily 6am–8pm	📞702 693 7472
Caesars Palace	Qua	Daily 6am–8pm	📞866 782 0655
The Cosmopolitan	Sahra	Daily 7am–8pm	📞702 698 7171
Encore	Spa	Daily 8am–8pm	📞702 770 4772
Golden Nugget	Spa	Daily 6am–8pm	📞702 386 8186
Hard Rock	Reliquary	Daily 8am–8pm	📞702 693 5520
Mandalay Bay	Bathhouse	Daily 6am–8.30pm	📞877 632 7300
The Mirage	Spa	Daily 6am–7pm	📞702 791 7146
Planet Hollywood	Mandara	Daily 7am–7pm	📞702 785 5772
The Venetian	Canyon Ranch	Daily 6am–8pm	📞702 414 3600
Wynn	Spa	Daily 8am–8pm	📞702 770 3900

is fundamentally the same as staying at the Venetian (once you go downstairs, you're in the same building), but you'll find yourself slightly further from the heart of the action. The actual rooms are very similar, with plush sleeping and living areas at slightly different levels, and huge marble bathrooms. **Resort fee $25/day. Mon–Thurs & Sun $209, Fri & Sat $299.**

PARIS > 3655 Las Vegas Blvd S ☎ 877 796 2096, ⊛ www.caesars.com /paris-las-vegas. MAP P.55, POCKET MAP G8 For many visitors, Paris represents an ideal compromise – you get to stay in an interesting big-name property, with excellent amenities plus "only in Vegas" features like the Eiffel Tower outside your window – without paying premium prices for opulent fittings you don't really need. The standard rooms are slightly faded now; for a little more pampering, opt for a newer "Red Room". **Resort fee $20/day. Mon–Thurs & Sun $93, Fri & Sat $201.**

PLANET HOLLYWOOD > 3667 Las Vegas Blvd S ☎ 800 342 7724, ⊛ www .caesars.com/planet-hollywood. MAP P.55, POCKET MAP G9 While Planet Hollywood's confusing layout can make it a long trek from your car to your room, once you're here it's a great-value central location. The rooms are in a style they call "Hollywood Hip", which tends to mean black and gold carpets and wallpaper; movie stills on the wall; and walk-in showers as well as baths. **Resort fee $20/day. Mon–Thurs & Sun $79, Fri & Sat $199.**

SLS LAS VEGAS > 2535 Las Vegas Blvd S ☎ 702 761 7757, ⊛ slslasvegas .com. MAP P.70, POCKET MAP L4 Despite standing well north of the Strip proper, the former Sahara is thriving enough to charge substantial rates for its nicely refurbished rooms. **Resort fee $25/day. Mon–Thurs & Sun $70, Fri & Sat $200**

THE STRATOSPHERE > 2000 Las Vegas Blvd S ☎ 800 998 6937 or ☎ 702 380 7777, ⊛ stratosphere hotel.com. MAP P.70, POCKET MAP L2 Much too far to walk to from either the Strip or downtown, the Stratosphere

is at least something of a destination in its own right – the rooms aren't in the 1000ft tower, but guests do get free admission. Find the right cut-price offer online, and its simple but sizeable rooms may suit your budget. **Resort fee $18/day. Mon–Thurs & Sun $31, Fri & Sat $75.**

TI (TREASURE ISLAND) > 3300 Las Vegas Blvd S ☎ 800 944 7444 or ☎ 702 894 7111, ⊛ treasureisland .com. MAP P.70, POCKET MAP G3 Like the building itself, the rooms at TI remain in good condition – they're nothing fancy, but they look reasonably fresh and have good beds – and the location is great too. These days, the whole place, and the pool in particular, attracts a young party crowd. Look out for online discounts. **Resort fee $25/ day. Mon–Thurs & Sun $69, Fri & Sat $149.**

THE TROPICANA > 3801 Las Vegas Blvd S ☎ 888 381 8767 or ☎ 702 739 2222, ⊛ www.troplv.com. MAP P.32, POCKET MAP C4 Completely overhauled in 2010, this long-standing landmark can't quite match its Mirage-owned neighbours for dining and nightlife, but seen simply as a place to stay, it offers large, cream-and-orange-rooms with new furnishings, an excellent pool complex and a location handy for the airport. **Resort fee $20/day. Mon–Thurs & Sun $99, Fri & Sat $179**

VDARA > 2600 W Harmon Ave ☎ 866 745 7767 or ☎ 702 590 2767, ⊛ vdara.com. MAP P.45, POCKET MAP E9 Hedonist holidaymakers might feel ill at ease with the austere steel-and-chrome aesthetic of this CityCenter all-suite hotel, and its lack of a casino, but if you're here to work, or just fancy an escape from Las Vegas's round-the-clock scene, it makes a peaceful and very comfortable retreat. **Resort fee $25/day. Mon–Thurs & Sun $114, Fri & Sat $180.**

THE VENETIAN > 3355 Las Vegas Blvd S ☎ 866 659 9643 or ☎ 702 414 1000, ⊛ www.venetian.com. MAP P.70, POCKET MAP G4 In terms of amenities in the property as a whole, and sheer comfort in its guest rooms, the Venetian ranks in the very top tier of Strip hotels; slightly more old-fashioned than Wynn, but still a true pampering experience. All the rooms are suites; you step down from the sleeping area, with its huge bed, to reach a sunken living space near the panoramic windows. Unusually, the price for advance bookings often remains the same for weekends as for weekdays. **Resort fee $20/day. Mon–Thurs & Sun $209, Fri & Sat $299.**

WYNN LAS VEGAS > 3131 Las Vegas Blvd S ☎877 321 9966 or ☎702 770 7000, ⓦwynnlasvegas.com. MAP P.70, POCKET MAP J2 With the arguable exception of the all-but-identical Encore alongside, this is as opulent as it gets in Vegas. The super-large rooms are tastefully decorated and equipped with luxurious linens, and bathrooms feature marble tubs, walk-in showers and even TVs. **Resort fee $25/day. Mon–Thurs & Sun $279, Fri & Sat $399.**

Downtown

THE D > 301 E Fremont St ☎702 388 2400, ⓦwww.thed.com. MAP P.87, POCKET MAP G12 Since turning from Fitzgerald's into The D, this central downtown hotel has become a real bargain. All its rooms have had a top-to-bottom makeover (each has two queen beds) and the amenities downstairs are much improved. The one problem can be noise from the Experience outside. **Resort fee $20/day. Mon–Thurs & Sun $29, Fri & Sat $99.**

EL CORTEZ > 600 E Fremont St ☎800 634 6703 or ☎702 385 5200, ⓦelcortezhotelcasino.com. MAP P.87, POCKET MAP H12 Long renowned as Las Vegas's cheapest casino, El Cortez stands a short but, at night, potentially intimidating walk from the heart of Fremont Street. Once there, everything's in good shape, though the "Vintage" rooms, reached via the stairs, are no better than faded motel rooms. The "Cabana" suites, across the street, are much more appealing. Online packages for first-time guests offset room rates with free meals and gaming. **Resort fee $9/day. Mon–Thurs & Sun $28, Fri & Sat $99.**

FOUR QUEENS > 202 E Fremont St ☎800 634 6045 or ☎702 385 4011, ⓦwww.fourqueens.com. MAP P.87, POCKET MAP G12 There's no real reason to pick this resolutely old-school downtown stalwart over any of its neighbours, though it has at least kept its rooms up to the adequate but unexciting level, say, of a $60-per-night national chain. **No resort fee. Mon–Thurs & Sun $39, Fri & Sat $99.**

FREMONT HOTEL > 200 E Fremont St ☎800 634 6182 or ☎702 385 3232, ⓦwww.fremontcasino.com. MAP P.87, POCKET MAP G12 As one of the few downtown casinos owned by a major corporation – Boyd Gaming – the Fremont keeps its standards pretty high. The rooms are small but up to date, with pleasant decor and linens, and it's really not a bad alternative if you fancy being in the thick of the Fremont Street action. **No resort fee. Mon–Thurs & Sun $38, Fri & Sat $100.**

THE GOLDEN GATE > 1 E Fremont St ☎800 426 1906 or ☎702 385 1906, ⓦgoldengatecasino.com. MAP P.87, POCKET MAP G11 Las Vegas's first ever hotel, one hundred years old in 2006, has been restyled as a 106-room "boutique hotel", with the promise that more suites will soon be added in a new extension. Yes, the rooms are small and the floors strangely lumpy, but you do get a true taste of Vegas history – plus, unfortunately, a blast of noise from the Experience. **Resort fee $20/day. Mon–Thurs & Sun $21, Fri & Sat $89.**

GOLDEN NUGGET > 129 E Fremont St ☎800 634 3454 or ☎702 385 7111, ⓦgoldennugget.com. MAP P.87, POCKET MAP G12 Downtown's classiest option is the only hotel hereabouts with amenities – like its amazing pool – to match the Strip giants. The actual rooms, at their freshest but loudest in the Rush Tower overlooking Fremont Street, are smart and comfortable, if not all that exciting. **Resort fee $5/day. Mon–Thurs & Sun $59, Fri & Sat $129.**

LAS VEGAS HOSTEL > 1322 E Fremont St ☎800 550 8958 or ☎702 385 1150, ⓦlasvegashostel.net. MAP P.87, POCKET MAP J13 Popular with young travellers, this converted motel is almost a mile east of downtown in an area where walking is unadvisable. Adequate bare-bones accommodation includes four-, six- and eight-bed single-sex and mixed dorms, and en-suite private rooms. There's also a pool, hot tub and organized activities. Wi-fi, parking and breakfast included. **Dorms $13–21/person; doubles $36.**

MAIN STREET STATION > 200 N Main St ☎ 800 465 0711 or ☎ 702 387 1896, Ⓦ www.mainstreetcasino.com. MAP P.87, POCKET MAP G11 A short but safe walk north of Fremont Street, this large and reasonably modern casino is always good value, for accommodation, food and drink; it's particularly good as an affordable base for a busy weekend. Ask for a room away from the interstate. **No resort fee. Mon–Thurs & Sun $38, Fri & Sat $100.**

THE PLAZA > 1 Main St ☎ 800 634 6575 or ☎ 702 386 2110, Ⓦ www .plazahotelcasino.com. MAP P.87, POCKET MAP F11 The veteran Plaza, at the end of Fremont Street on the site of Las Vegas's original railroad station, pulled off a real coup in 2011. It bought up the brand-new fixtures and fittings from the prestigious Fontainebleu on the Strip, so badly hit by the recession it never even opened, and used them to turn its rundown rooms into some of the smartest and best value lodgings around. **Resort fee $11/day. Mon–Thurs & Sun $40, Fri & Sat $99.**

The rest of the city

GOLD COAST >4000 W Flamingo Rd, ☎ 888 402 6278 or ☎ 702 367 7111, Ⓦ www.goldcoastcasino.com. MAP P.95, POCKET MAP G15 Sedate, old-fashioned locals casino, complete with bingo and a bowling alley, a hot half-mile west of the Strip (to which it's connected by free shuttle buses), but right by the fancier Rio and Palms. The rooms are not at all bad, but there's no earthly reason to stay unless the price is right. **Resort fee $10/day. Mon–Thurs & Sun $55, Fri & Sat $114.**

HARD ROCK HOTEL > 4455 Paradise Rd ☎ 800 473 7625, Ⓦ www.hardrock hotel.com. MAP P.95, POCKET MAP B16 If you know what you're coming for – to mix with partying 20-somethings – the *Hard Rock* will suit you perfectly. The rooms are cool and comfortable, and you can even open the floor-to-ceiling windows. It's too far from the Strip, though, to make a good base for seeing the city as a whole. Weekends book up early; reserve in advance. **Resort fee $22/day. Mon–Thurs & Sun $67, Fri & Sat $199.**

ORLEANS > 4500 W Tropicana Ave ☎ 800 675 3267 or ☎ 702 365 7111, Ⓦ www.orleanscasino.com. MAP P.95, POCKET MAP A12 Provided you get one of its freshly renovated rooms and you have a car to get around, the Orleans, a mile west of the Strip, can serve as an affordable base to explore Las Vegas. The on-site cinema is a real boon. **Resort fee $10/day. Mon–Thurs & Sun $50, Fri & Sat $115.**

THE PALMS > 4321 W Flamingo Rd ☎866 942 7777 or ☎702 942 7777, Ⓦpalms.com. MAP P.95, POCKET MAP F16 One of the very few off-Strip casinos that you might genuinely want to stay in, rather than simply find a good-value rate for, the Palms is renowned for its clubs, gigs and weekend buzz. Things are much quieter on weekdays, but with such comfortable rooms and great pools, it can be a real bargain. **Resort fee $25/day. Mon–Thurs & Sun $89, Fri & Sat $169.**

RIO > 3700 W Flamingo Rd ☎866 746 7671, Ⓦwww.caesars.com/rio-las -vegas. MAP P.95, POCKET MAP H15 Part of the Caesars Entertainment empire, but separated by half a mile from its Strip siblings, the Rio really isn't a bad accommodation option. As well as high-class amenities and entertainment, it offers comfortable rooms (large but not suites, as they claim). The Palms is over the road, but you may feel you're missing out on all the action. **Resort fee $20/day. Mon–Thurs & Sun $69, Fri & Sat $149.**

SAM'S TOWN > 5111 Boulder Hwy ☎ 800 897 8696 or ☎ 702 456 7777, Ⓦ www.samstownlv.com. MAP P.95, POCKET MAP D12 Quietly prospering from meeting its middle-American customers' needs with Wild-West shops, restaurants and NASCAR races, this old-fashioned locals casino stands resolutely apart from modern Las Vegas. If you want to dip into town but stay somewhere more peaceful, its comfortable rooms may suit you fine. It's a six-mile shuttle ride to the Strip so you're better off with a car. **Resort fee $10/day. Mon–Thurs & Sun $33, Fri & Sat $99.**

SUNSET STATION > 1301 W Sunset Rd, Henderson ☏ 888 786 7389 or ☏ 702 547 7777, ⓦ sunsetstation.com. MAP P.95, POCKET MAP D13 This huge, attractive and well-equipped casino, ten miles southeast of the Strip en route towards Arizona, would seem impressive anywhere else. Here, despite its pool and fine restaurants, it counts as low-key, and only worth considering if the price is right or you're passing through. **Resort fee $15/day. Mon–Thurs & Sun $40, Fri & Sat $114.**

WESTGATE LAS VEGAS RESORT > 3000 Paradise Rd ☏ 702 732 5111, ⓦ westgateresorts.com. MAP P.95, POCKET MAP L5 How the mighty are fallen. The only reason to stay in the former Hilton – once, as home to Elvis, Las Vegas's premier hotel – is if you're attending a convention next door. Otherwise, the rooms just aren't good enough to compensate for the cut-off location and general air of decay. **Resort fee $20/day. Mon–Thurs & Sun $98, Fri & Sat $134.**

Mount Charleston

MOUNT CHARLESTON LODGE > 5375 Kyle Canyon Rd ☏ 702 872 5408, ⓦ mtcharlestonlodge.com. MAP PP.104–105 Nineteen comfortably appointed log cabins, alongside the restaurant (see p.111) at the far end of Hwy-157. Lacking phones, wi-fi and TV reception, they're especially popular with honeymooners escaping Las Vegas. **$125.**

RESORT ON MOUNT CHARLESTON > 2 Kyle Canyon Rd ☏ 888 559 1888, ☏ 702 872 5500, ⓦ mtcharlestonresort.com. MAP PP.104–105 Set below Hwy-157, facing a towering rocky outcrop 17 miles up from US-95, the best accommodation option in the mountains holds 61 cosy, smart rooms, arranged around an artificial lake. **$95.**

Grand Canyon South Rim

BRIGHT ANGEL LODGE > Grand Canyon South Rim, AZ. Advance reservations ☏ 888 297 2757 or ☏ 303 297 2757, same-day reservations ☏ 928 638 2631, ⓦ grandcanyonlodges.com. MAP PP.104–105 Stretching along the South Rim and consisting of a grand lodge flanked by individual cabins, this fantastic-value option is usually booked up months in advance. Some units share bathrooms, while others enjoy canyon views. **Double with shared bathroom $83.**

EL TOVAR > Grand Canyon South Rim, AZ. Advance reservations ☏ 888 297 2757 or ☏ 303 297 2757, same-day reservations ☏ 928 638 2631, ⓦ www.grandcanyonlodges.com. MAP PP.104–105 At heart an overgrown log cabin, this magnificent, century-old hotel, a symphony in dark wood, is the definitive national park lodge. Although it's very close to the rim, only three of its 78 rooms offer substantial canyon views. **$188.**

Zion National Park

DESERT PEARL INN > 707 Zion Park Blvd, Springdale UT ☏ 888 828 0898 or ☏ 435 772 8888, ⓦ desertpearl.com. MAP PP.104–105 An absolutely gorgeous hotel, ranged alongside the Virgin River just outside the park, with superb views. From the parking areas it may look like a regular motel, but the actual rooms are huge, modern and very attractive, and there's a good pool with hot tubs. **$158.**

ZION LODGE > Zion National Park, UT. Advance reservations ☏ 888 297 2757 or ☏ 303 297 2757, same-day reservations ☏ 435 772 7700, ⓦ www.zionlodge.com. MAP PP.104–105 The only accommodation option inside the national park, occupying pride of place on lush lawns in the heart of the Canyon. The forty en-suite cabins have gas fireplaces and private porches, while the 72 motel rooms are plainer, but still have porches or balconies. **Motel rooms $196, cabins $199.**

Arrival

A very high proportion of visitors to Las Vegas **fly** into the city's only significant airport, not far east of the Strip, while all the rest **drive** across the empty desert from elsewhere in the USA. No passenger trains currently serve the city, though there's talk of constructing a high-speed link with Los Angeles.

By air

Las Vegas's ever-expanding **McCarran International Airport** (☎702 261 5211, ⊕www.mccarran .com) lies immediately southeast of the Strip; aircraft pass within a mile of Mandalay Bay and the Tropicana as they taxi. However, both its terminals – confusingly numbered 1 and 3, since the new Terminal 3, used by all international flights, replaced the former Terminal 2 in 2012 – are accessed from the east, via Paradise Road. That means the closest Strip casinos are around three miles by road from the airport; the Venetian and Wynn more like five miles; and downtown hotels around seven miles.

Assuming you're not renting a car – in which case, note that all the rental companies are based at a separate, off-site facility (see p.126) – much the best way to transfer from the airport to your hotel is by **taxi**. In principle, a cab ride to the southern Strip (10–20min) will cost $16 and upwards, and to the northern Strip (20–30min) more like $30. If the traffic's bad you may have to pay up to $10 more.

Lone travellers may prefer to pay for a seat in a shared **Bell Trans shuttle bus** (☎702 739 7990, ⊕bell -trans.com), which costs $7.50 to the Strip and $10 to downtown, but as these services drop off other passengers en route the journey time can be long, an hour or more for properties on the North Strip.

It is also possible, but even slower, to use the **RTC bus network** (see p.125), by taking route #109 from the airport to the South Strip Transfer Terminal, and changing there onto the Strip And Downtown Express, for a total fare of $3. The total journey is likely to take at least half an hour for the South Strip, and over an hour for the North Strip and downtown.

Note that the **Las Vegas Monorail** (see p.126) does not serve the airport.

By car

The main driving route into Las Vegas is the **I-15** interstate, which connects the city with Los Angeles, 270 miles southwest, and Salt Lake City, 420 miles northeast. On Fridays especially, it tends to be clogged with cars arriving from southern California. Only if traffic is at a standstill is it worth leaving the interstate before you reach the exit closest to your final destination. If you're coming from California, therefore, you wouldn't normally expect to drive the full length of Las Vegas Boulevard, which runs parallel to I-15 from the southern end of the valley, and becomes the Strip roughly ten miles along.

Driving to Las Vegas from the Grand Canyon or anywhere else in Arizona, you'll approach the city along **US-93**, via the Hoover Dam. Either follow the same road, as Boulder Highway, all the way to downtown, or turn west, most likely on Tropicana Road or Flamingo Avenue, to reach the Strip.

By bus

Long-distance **Greyhound buses** (☎800 231 2222, ⊕www.greyhound .com), which connect Las Vegas with other Southwestern cities including Los Angeles, Phoenix and Salt Lake City, stop downtown rather than on the Strip. The station is alongside the Plaza hotel, at 200 S Main Street.

Getting around

If you're visiting Las Vegas specifically to spend time on the Strip and/or downtown – as is the case for most visitors – there's no point renting a car. Downtown is small enough to walk around, while a good **bus service** runs the full length of the Strip and continues to downtown, and there are also several separate **monorail systems** on the Strip. Only if you expect to explore any further afield, whether to outlying areas (see p.94), or to the surrounding desert (see p.104), does a car become essential.

On foot

It comes as a big surprise to most visitors quite how much **walking** you have to do in Las Vegas. The Strip might look like a simple straight line on the map, but it has a peculiar geography all its own; the colossal scale of the buildings tricks the eye, making them look smaller and nearer than they really are. Each individual casino can measure a mile end to end, while walking from, say, a restaurant in one property to a club in the next can take half an hour. Especially in summer, when the searing heat makes it all but impossible to walk more than a block or two outdoors, plotting a route from A to B becomes a real art, involving cutting through air-conditioned casinos, catching the occasional monorail and other such dodges.

By bus

While **RTC buses** (ⓦcatride.com) cover the whole city, two main routes meet the needs of almost all visitors. You must buy a ticket before you board; vending machines at stops along both routes sell a 2-hour pass for $6, a 24-hour pass for $8 or a 3-day pass for $20. All buses are wheelchair accessible.

The **Deuce on the Strip** (daily 24hr) runs the full length of the Strip, from Mandalay Bay to the Stratosphere, stopping outside all the casinos, and also loops around downtown, running north on Casino Center Boulevard and south on Las Vegas Boulevard. While its principal downtown stop is where the Fremont Street Experience meets Las Vegas Boulevard, it also stops in both directions at the Bonneville Transit Center (BTC), six blocks south at Bonneville and Casino Center, the main interchange for crosstown routes.

As the name suggests, the faster **Strip & Downtown Express**, or SDX, (daily 9am–midnight) also connects the Strip with downtown, but with fewer stops. In addition, rather than follow the Strip between Wynn Las Vegas and the Stratosphere, it detours west to run past the Convention Center. Downtown, the most useful stop is where the Fremont Street Experience meets Casino Center Boulevard, though the route loops back west beyond Fremont Street to terminate at the Las Vegas Premium Outlets (North) mall, and it also stops at the Bonneville Transit Center. Southbound SDX buses stop on the Strip outside the Fashion Show Mall, Bellagio, Excalibur and Mandalay Bay; northbound buses stop across from Mandalay Bay, and outside the MGM Grand, Paris and Wynn. The southern end of the route is the South Strip Transfer Terminal (SSTT), three miles southeast of Mandalay Bay at 6675 Gilespie Street, which connects with other bus routes and is also served by free airport shuttle buses.

In addition, various free **shuttle buses** connect the Strip with further-flung casinos. From Harrah's, buses run west to the Rio (half-hourly departures, daily 10am–1am; ☎800 214 9110) and east to Sam's Town (every 1hr 30min, daily 9.30am–9.30pm; ☎800 897 8696). From the intersection of Flamingo Road with the Strip, buses run via the Gold Coast to the Orleans (half-hourly departures, daily 9.30am–12.30am).

By monorail

Four separate monorail systems currently operate along different stretches of the Strip. The longest, but in some respects least useful, is the one officially called the **Las Vegas Monorail** (Mon–Thurs 7am–2am, Fri–Sun 7am–3am; single trip $5, 1-day pass $12, 3-day pass $28; ⓦwww.lvmonorail.com). It runs behind the casinos on the eastern side of the Strip, from the MGM Grand to SLS Las Vegas, detouring east en route to call at the Convention Center. Had the route been extended south to the airport, and downtown in the north, it could have relieved Las Vegas's traffic problems. As it is, it's only conceivably helpful for hops along the southern Strip. Even then, all the stations are located right at the back of the relevant casinos, ten minutes' walk from their Strip entrances, so it can be slower to catch the Monorail than to walk.

All the other three monorail systems are **free**, and link small groups of neighbouring casinos. The southernmost connects Mandalay Bay with Excalibur, via Luxor. The second runs from the Monte Carlo, via Aria and Crystals in CityCenter, to Bellagio; it's a futuristic ride, but be warned the Bellagio station is in that property's far southwestern corner, far from the casino floor and the Strip. Finally, the short link between the Mirage and TI now serves little practical function other than keeping pedestrians cool.

By car

Locals might find it hard to believe, but for visitors, **driving** in Las Vegas can be a real pleasure. The thrill of cruising along the Strip, with its sights and sounds and blazing signs, only wears thin if you're actually trying to get somewhere by a certain time. Tourists tend naturally to avoid the worst times for traffic, like the morning rush hour.

Along the Strip, every casino offers **free parking**, albeit in an enormous multistorey garage around the back – somewhere that may well be a long walk from your destination. You can save a lot of time by using valet parking at the main entrance; in theory it's free, but you're expected to tip around $2. Most downtown casinos charge non-guests a parking fee, but it's often waived if you spend money in their restaurants or bars.

Car rental is available from almost every Strip or downtown hotel; as a rule each holds one or two outlets of the major rental chains. However, you can find a much wider choice, and usually better rates, if you pick up at the airport. That said, the major rental agencies are no longer based at the airport itself, but at the **McCarran Rent-A-Car Center**, three miles southwest at 7135 Gilespie Street, which is connected with the terminals by free shuttle buses. If you're already in the city and decide to rent a car, be sure to take a cab direct to the Rent-A-Car Center. Whether you book via the agencies' own websites, or online brokers like Travelocity or Expedia, you can expect to pay around $40 per day, or $200 per week, for a compact car.

By taxi

You can't hail a passing **taxi** on the street in Las Vegas, but long lines of cabs wait to pick up passengers at the casino entrances, as well as at the airport. Meters calculate fares on the basis of $3.30 for the first mile and $2.60 for each additional mile, but also run if you're delayed in traffic, charging $1 every two minutes. There's an additional $2 surcharge for trips to or from the airport (see p.124). Fifteen percent is the usual tip for the driver.

Gambling

Gambling, or as they like to call it these days "**gaming**", lies at the root of everything in Las Vegas. Only one visitor in ten doesn't gamble at all; the rest lose an average of $500 each in the casinos. Whether you're pumping coins into a slot machine or trying to beat the dealer at blackjack, the rules always mean the casino enjoys the "house edge". So long as you're 21 or over, and carrying ID to prove it, you can gamble anywhere you like. The glamour of the large **Strip casinos** can be seductive, but the minimum stake for each game tends to be higher, and the odds a little worse. Many visitors prefer to gamble **downtown**, where the atmosphere is a bit more down-and-dirty and their money holds out longer. Either way, decide in advance how much you're prepared to lose, and stop if you reach that point.

In all casinos waitresses will ply you with free drinks as long as you are gambling; tips are expected. If you gamble for any length of time, join the casino's free players club; it can earn you meals, freebies and future stays.

Baccarat

Formerly the preserve of high-rolling "whales", **baccarat** (pronounced bah-kah-rah) accounts for over forty percent of the casinos' revenue from table games. Played with an ordinary pack in which each numbered card counts its face value (aces are 1 not 11), except tens, jacks, queens and kings, all valued at zero, it's a simple game of luck. Only two hands are dealt, the "player" and the "bank". Each aims to reach a total value of nine; you can bet on either, but the bank has a slightly better chance of winning. The house advantage comes because the casino rakes off a small commission.

Blackjack

Also known as "21" or "pontoon", **blackjack** remains Las Vegas's favourite card game. Players compete against the bank, attempting to build a hand that adds nearly, or exactly, to 21. Tens, jacks, queens and kings count as ten points, aces as either one or eleven. Players make their bets before receiving two cards, then each in turn plays their hand through to completion, saying "hit" to receive additional cards, and either "stand" to stop, or "bust" if the total exceeds 21. The dealer plays last, according to fixed rules that preclude individual judgement. The house advantage comes because players who go bust lose their stakes whether or not the dealer does too. Players can minimize that advantage by learning the "correct" response to every situation – it's so hard that some casinos happily provide gamblers with the relevant charts.

Craps

If you don't know how to play the dice game **craps**, played on a high-walled baize table, take a lesson (freely available in most casinos) – you'll never be able to learn it from watching. The basic idea is that a different "shooter" throws a pair of dice each time around. Players bet on either "pass" or "don't pass" before the first throw, known as the "come-out roll". If that throw is 7 or 11, "pass" has won; if it's 2, 3 or 12, "don't pass" wins. Anything else, and the shooter throws again, and keeps doing so until either matching the original throw – a win for "pass" – or throwing 7 – a win for "don't pass". All sorts of side bets capture the imaginations of serious gamblers.

Poker

In **poker**, players compete against each other, not the house, to build the best five-card hand (see box, p.128). The two most popular variations are

Seven Card Stud, in which each player receives two cards face down, four face up, and then the last face down, and Texas Hold 'Em, in which your two face-down cards are supplemented by five face-up communal cards. The casino rakes off a percentage of each pot. You're therefore playing against whoever else happens to be around; it's possible to win, but it's a big risk to assume you're the best player at the table.

Casinos also offer what's effectively poker played in a **blackjack format**, in which each player attempts to beat the dealer. Formats include Let It Ride, Pai Gow Poker and Caribbean Stud.

Roulette
Roulette is the game in which a ball lands in a numbered slot in a rotating wheel. You can bet on the specific number, or group of numbers, and if the slot is "red" or "black". Winners are paid as though the wheel holds 36 slots, but it usually holds 38, thanks to two green slots, 0 and 00. Always look for wheels that hold only one extra slot, and thus offer better odds. You can't get your money back by repeatedly redoubling your stake; tables allow bets up to a quickly reached maximum.

Slot machines
Casinos make more money from **slot machines** than from anything else. All machines are programmed to pay out a percentage of their intake as winnings. On average, visitors feed $1600 per day into every single machine in the city, and win $1500 back again, leaving the casino $100 profit. The slots downtown offer better odds than on the Strip.

A "non-progressive" machine always pays the same for a specific winning combination and pays smaller but more frequent jackpots. "Progressive" slots, such as Wheel of Fortune, are linked into networks where the overall jackpot can climb into millions of dollars, before someone scoops the lot.

Video poker is an addictive cross between traditional slot machines and the table game. The odds can be so good that on certain machines, players who play a perfect strategy have a slight advantage over the house.

Sports betting
Las Vegas is all but unique in the USA in offering visitors the chance to bet on sports events legally, in the highly charged atmosphere of a major casino. Almost every casino holds either a **Sports Book**, or if it covers horseracing as well, a Race and Sports Book, which vary from comfortable high-tech lounges to something more like a raucous neighbourhood sports bar. All offer much the same odds on any specific event and many offer "in-running" wagering, meaning moment-by-moment bets on games currently in progress.

Ranking of poker hands
Straight flush Five consecutive cards in the same suit.
Four of a kind Four aces, four sevens, etc.
Full house Three of a kind and a separate pair.
Flush Any five cards in the same suit.
Straight Five consecutive cards not in the same suit.
Three of a kind Three Kings, three sixes, etc.
Two pair Two fours and two Jacks, etc.
One pair Two tens, etc.

Directory A–Z

Cinemas

Typical ticket prices for cinemas in Las Vegas are around $8 for matinee performances, starting before 6pm, and $10 for evening shows.

AMC Town Square 18 Town Square, 6587 Las Vegas Blvd S ☎702 362 7283, ⓦwww.amctheatres.com.

Brenden Theatres & IMAX The Palms, 4321 W Flamingo Rd ☎702 507 4849, ⓦwww.brendentheatres.com.

Century 18 Orleans, 4500 W Tropicana Ave ☎702 889 1220, ⓦwww.cinemark.com.

Century 18 Sam's Town, 5111 Boulder Hwy ☎702 547 1732, ⓦwww.cinemark.com.

Regal 13 Sunset Station, 1301 W Sunset Rd, Henderson ☎702 221 2283, ⓦwww.regmovies.com.

United Artists Showcase 8 Next door to the MGM Grand at 3769 Las Vegas Blvd S ☎702 221 2283, ⓦwww.regmovies.com. The only cinema on the Strip.

Crime

While you're safe in the major public spaces of Las Vegas, such as inside the security-conscious casinos, crime can be a problem elsewhere. Away from the crowded Strip, which has its own problems with **pickpockets** and bag-snatchers, you can feel exposed and vulnerable if you walk any distance outdoors. It's essential to keep your cash hidden at all times, not to flaunt valuables like cameras and iPads, and not to tell strangers your hotel room number. Be cautious in multistorey parking garages, especially at night, and try to park close to the exits.

Electricity

The **electricity** supply in Las Vegas, as in all of the USA, is 110 volts AC, and uses two-pin plugs. Bring or buy an adapter, and if necessary a voltage converter as well, if you're travelling from a country that uses a different system and need to use your own electrical appliances.

Gay and lesbian travellers

Although Las Vegas, or at least the parts of the city that visitors are at all likely to see, is a **gay-friendly** city, the casinos make little show of catering to gay travellers in any specific sense. **Liaison**, in Bally's, is the only gay club in a Strip casino. Otherwise, the city's gay-oriented nightlife is focused around what's fondly known as the "**Fruit Loop**", a mile east of the Strip, where Paradise Road, running south from the Hard Rock, meets Naples Drive. Well-known clubs in the neighbourhood include Piranha (see p.103), but there are none exclusively geared towards women.

The best source of information on current issues and events in Las Vegas's gay community is the monthly magazine *QVegas*, distributed in a free printed version and also available online (ⓦqvegas.com).

Since same-sex marriage was declared legal in Nevada in 2014, the major casino chapels have rushed to offer gay wedding ceremonies, even if certain private chapels have refused. The **Gay Chapel of Las Vegas**, 1205 Las Vegas Blvd S (☎702 384 0771, ⓦgaychapeloflasvegas.com) offers a full range of ceremonies; Elvis is optional.

The annual **Las Vegas Pride** event, celebrated in early September (☎866 930 3336, ⓦlasvegaspride.org), kicks off with a Friday-night parade through downtown, while the Saturday sees an open-air festival in the grounds of the Clark County Government Center, a few blocks southwest.

In May, the **Nevada Gay Rodeo Association** (ⓦngra.com) holds the three-day BigHorn Rodeo at Horse-man's Park, 5800 E Flamingo Rd.

Health

In any medical emergency, call ☎911. The front desk or phone operator at your hotel will be able to advise on sources of appropriate help. **Hospitals** that have 24hr emergency rooms include Sunrise Hospital, 3186 S Maryland Parkway (☎702 731 8000, ⊛sunrisehospital.com), and the University Medical Center, 1800 W Charleston Blvd (☎702 383 2000, ⊛www.umcsn.com). For more minor issues, head to the Harmon Medical Center, 150 E Harmon Ave (Mon–Fri 8am–8pm; ☎702 796 1116).

Twenty-four-hour **pharmacies** on the Strip include the 24hr CVS Pharmacy, alongside the Monte Carlo at 3758 Las Vegas Blvd S (☎702 262 9284) and Walgreens, beside the main Palazzo entrance at 3339 Las Vegas Blvd S (☎702 369 8166).

To find a local **dentist**, contact the Nevada Dental Association (☎702 255 4211, ⊛nvda.org).

Internet

Every casino/hotel in Las Vegas provides in-room **wi-fi** access for its guests, but only rarely is it free. In almost all cases, internet access forms the largest component of the compulsory "resort fee" (see box, p.115), which typically costs at least $20 per day, and may well cover one device only; elsewhere, hotel guests can generally choose to pay a stand-alone fee of around $15 per day. On top of that, if you're spending time in a casino other than one you're staying in, you won't normally have wi-fi access.

Several casinos however, including most of the MGM Resorts properties, offer **free wi-fi** access to everyone in their public areas, as opposed to the guest rooms. In addition, a handful of shops and cafés along the Strip provide free wi-fi to customers (and anyone who happens to be in the immediate vicinity): *Coffee Bean & Tea Leaf* in Planet Hollywood's Miracle Mile (see p.62); *Kahunaville* in TI (see p.81); and the Apple Store and *Starbucks* in the Fashion Show Mall (see p.77).

There is wi-fi is also available throughout McCarran International Airport.

Money

Las Vegas is not a budget destination in any meaningful sense. The days are gone when casinos used cut-price food and entertainment to lure in gamblers. Now everything from restaurants to showrooms have to make a profit, and prices are high. A typical all-you-can-eat buffet costs $20 or more for dinner; a run-of-the-mill restaurant more like $40 per head, without drinks; and a gourmet place double that or more. Tickets for a show can easily cost $100 or more, while a night out in a big club is liable to cost hundreds, and potentially thousands, of dollars. Hotel room rates are generally good value, and on weekdays compare favourably with what you'd get for the same money elsewhere in the USA, but can run into hundreds per night on weekends. On top of that, of course, the average visitor also loses several hundred dollars gambling.

As for how you bring your money, it's totally assumed you'll use a **credit card** for all significant expenses. It's extremely easy to get cash anywhere on the Strip; ATMs are everywhere, though all tend to charge around $3 for withdrawals.

Travellers from overseas are advised not to bring foreign cash; there are no banks on the Strip, and while the casinos will gladly change your cash you won't get a good rate. Dollar **travellers'** cheques are accepted as cash everywhere, though few visitors bring them these days.

Phones

Foreign visitors can assume that their **mobile phones** (cellphones) will work in Las Vegas, though it's worth checking with your phone provider that your existing payment scheme will cover you there, and what the call charges are. Many providers offer short-term pricing packages designed to make holiday phone usage more affordable. If you plan to access the internet using your phone, make sure you know your provider's roaming charges, which may well be extremely expensive.

For all calls, you can make tremendous savings by using **Skype**, or similar programmes, to make free wi-fi calls from your phone or laptop. Alternatively, prepaid **phone cards** are widely available from casino convenience stores, petrol (gas) stations, supermarkets and other outlets. Many casinos, especially those that charge resort fees (see p.115), offer guests free local phone calls; making an international call from your hotel room phone is always liable to be very expensive.

Smoking

Smoking remains legal in the public areas of all casinos, and in bars that do not serve food. It is forbidden in restaurants, including those inside casinos, though smoke does waft into those restaurants that are open to the casino floor. All hotels offer non-smoking rooms.

Tax

Sales tax of 8.1 percent is charged on all purchases in Las Vegas. Hotel rates are subject to an additional **room tax** of twelve percent on the Strip, and thirteen percent downtown (see box, p.115).

Time

Las Vegas is in the **Pacific Time Zone**, three hours behind the Eastern Time Zone. It's almost always seven hours behind the UK, though clocks in the US move forward by one hour on the second Sunday in March and back one hour on the first Sunday in November, placing them briefly out of synch with clocks in the UK.

Tipping

Tipping etiquette is not as complicated as many visitors imagine; if you find yourself wondering whether to tip, do. Servers in restaurants depend on tips for their income, and expect at least fifteen percent. So do cab drivers. If someone carries your bags, tip $1–2 per bag; valet parking attendants expect $2; and it's usual to leave a tip of $1 or $2 per day when you leave your hotel room. When gambling, it's considered appropriate to tip the dealer a chip or two if you win. Bar staff, or casino waitresses bringing free drinks, expect $1–2 per drink.

Tourist information

The best single source of information on the city is ⓦvisitlasvegas .com, the website of the **Las Vegas Convention and Visitor Authority** (LVCVA). They also run a visitor centre at 3150 Paradise Rd, half a mile east of the Strip (Mon–Fri 8am–5pm; ☎877 847 4858), but it holds nothing you can't find much more easily elsewhere.

Other useful websites include: ⓦ**www.eatinglv.com** This long-running blog holds a huge archive of restaurant reviews.

ⓦwww.everythinglv.com Weekly online updates on the latest Las Vegas news, plus reader forums.

ⓦlasvegascitylife.com The website of the free weekly City Life magazine; useful for news as well as current listings.

ⓦlasvegassun.com Las Vegas's best daily newspaper website.

ⓦlasvegasweekly.com A good source of current listings.

ⓦwww.lvol.com Schedules, reservations and reviews for concerts and shows; a good place to find out what's happening while you're in town.

ⓦwww.vegaschatter.com Lively gossip about Las Vegas comings and goings.

Travellers with disabilities

The **Las Vegas Convention and Visitors Authority** offers detailed advice for disabled visitors; download the Access Las Vegas brochure from ⓦvisitlasvegas.co.uk, or call their advice line on ☎702 892 0711.

All the casinos in Las Vegas are **wheelchair accessible** and offer hotel rooms designed to suit visitors with disabilities. Don't underestimate the sheer scale of each casino, let alone the Strip as a whole; an individual destination like a restaurant or a theatre may be a long way from the nearest parking space. If you need to rent specific mobility equipment, contact Ability Center, 6001 S Decatur Blvd (☎702 434 3030, ⓦwww.ability center.com). For public transport, both Bell Trans shuttle buses from the airport (☎702 739 7990, ⓦbell-trans. com) and RTC buses in the city itself (ⓦcatride.com) are wheelchair accessible. If you plan to drive yourself, the national rental chains offer adapted vehicles, and visitors can arrange temporary free **disabled parking**

permits via the Nevada Department of Motor Vehicles (☎775 684 4750, ⓦwww.dmvnv.com).

Tours

Las Vegas does not offer the kind of **sightseeing tours** familiar in other cities. Almost everything of interest in the city itself is in and around the casinos; you can't really appreciate them from a passing bus, and they're too big to explore more than one or two at a time on foot. **Bus tours** do however head further afield. Thus Gray Line (☎702 739 7777, ⓦwww .grayline.com) offers tours to the Hoover Dam (4hr 30min; $65); the Grand Canyon West Rim (11hr; $149); and the Grand Canyon South Rim (14hr; $175). Helicopter operators, including Maverick (☎702 261 0007, ⓦwww.maverickhelicopter .com) and Sundance (☎702 736 0606, ⓦwww.sundancehelicopters .com), offer brief day or night **"flightseeing" tours** over the Strip, at typical prices of around $100 for a flight lasting less than fifteen minutes. They and other companies also fly day trippers east to the Grand Canyon (see box, p.108).

Travelling with children

In the early 1990s, Las Vegas flirted briefly with the idea that it might become a child-friendly destination to match Orlando, Florida. That dream was swiftly abandoned; gambling and kids don't make a good mix. Even so, many visitors bring their **kids** to the city; the Strip sidewalk is thronged until after midnight with parents pushing cumbersome buggies and struggling with exhausted children.

There's still a lot about Las Vegas that will appeal to kids, from the castles and pyramids, volcanoes and fountains on the Strip, to more specific paying attractions. Among the most popular with children are the Secret Garden and Dolphin Habitat at the Mirage; Shark Reef at Mandalay Bay; the Bodies and Titanic exhibitions at Luxor; the gondolas at the Venetian; CSI: The Experience at the MGM Grand; and the roller coasters and thrill rides at New York–New York, Circus Circus and the Stratosphere.

All the casinos welcome children as guests. Strictly speaking, **under-21s** are not allowed in gambling areas, which means that family groups have to keep walking rather than linger on the casino floor. Casinos do not offer babysitting services, but can provide details of babysitting agencies.

Note that in many casinos, some or all the swimming pools now operate as adults-only "dayclubs", with drinking, dancing and partying; it's worth checking in advance before you go ahead and book your accommodation.

Weddings

Thanks to Nevada's notoriously minimal legal requirements, and especially the lack of an obligatory waiting period, around a quarter of a million people get married in Las Vegas each year.

At its simplest, arranging a Vegas wedding is very straightforward. First of all, you need a **Nevada marriage licence**. To get that, both parties must appear in person at the Clark County Marriage Bureau, 201 E Clark Ave, downtown (daily 8am–midnight; ☎702 671 0600, ⍟www .clarkcountynv.gov). So long as both are aged 18 or over, not married already and can show picture ID, they'll sell you a licence for $60 (credit cards $65, debit cards not accepted). Note that there isn't an office on the Strip.

If you've made an advance reservation, you can then walk with your licence to the office of the **Commissioner of Civil Marriages**, on the sixth floor at 330 S Third St (Mon–Thurs & Sun 2–6pm, Fri 10am–9pm, Sat 12.30–9pm; ☎702 671 0577, ⍟www.clarkcountynv.gov) and pay another $50 cash to have the actual ceremony performed. One witness is required; ideally you should bring your own, though what the Commissioner charmingly calls "unsavoury individuals" lurk outside the offices, hoping to sell their services as witnesses.

Just because it's possible to have a quick, cheap wedding in Las Vegas, however, doesn't mean that's what most couples actually do. Instead, most marriages are celebrated in wedding chapels, which can be stand-alone structures of the kind reviewed throughout this book or yet another component in the huge casino-hotels. You can find full listings of chapels and wedding planners on the official Las Vegas CVB website, ⍟www.lasvegas .com, and also on the casinos' own websites.

Prices at **wedding chapels** range upwards from around $200 all-in for a bare-bones ceremony. For the full works, which in Las Vegas can include helicopter flights to the Grand Canyon or pretty much anything else you care to mention, the bill can of course run into thousands of dollars. The biggest hidden expense is likely to be photography; be sure to check whether you or your guests will be allowed to bring cameras, and if not, how much the official photos or footage will cost.

Finally, note that now **gay marriage** has become legal in Nevada all the major casino chapels, and most but not all of the private chapels, are happy to perform gay weddings. For more details, see p.129.

133

Festivals

Compared to other American cities, Las Vegas does not have an extensive calendar of annual events. In terms of attracting crowds, the biggest events tend to be the opening of new casinos and, even more exciting, the implosions of old ones.

NASCAR WEEKEND

Early March ⓦwww.lvms.com
Three days of racing at the Las Vegas Motor Speedway, 7000 Las Vegas Blvd N at Speedway Blvd.

ST PATRICK'S DAY

March 17
Pubs, clubs, casinos and restaurants all celebrate St Patrick's Day.

WORLD SERIES OF POKER

Late May to mid-July ⓦpoker.wsop.com
The world's premier poker tournament has been held at the Rio since 1995.

LAS VEGAS HELLDORADO DAYS

Mid-May ⓦwww.elkshelldorado.com
Five nights of pro rodeo action in

Public holidays

Jan 1 New Year's Day
Jan 15 Martin Luther King Jr's Birthday
3rd Mon in Feb Presidents' Day
Last Mon in May Memorial Day
July 4 Independence Day
1st Mon in Sept Labor Day
2nd Mon in Oct Columbus Day
Nov 11 Veterans' Day
Last Thurs in Nov Thanksgiving Day
Dec 25 Christmas Day

Symphony Park – at 100 S Grand Central Parkway, alongside downtown's Smith Center – plus a Saturday night parade downtown.

NATIONAL FINALS RODEO

Early Dec ⓦnfrexperience.com
Ten-day pro rodeo event at the Thomas & Mack Center, 4505 S Maryland Parkway.

NEW YEAR'S EVE

December 31
The biggest night in the city's calendar, marked by concerts and festivities.

Conventions and trade shows

When planning a visit, it's useful to know when the city's biggest **conventions** are happening as room rates can soar.

Mid-Jan Consumer Electronics Show

Mid-Feb Men's Apparel Guild (MAGIC) convention

Early April National Association of Broadcasters convention

Mid-Aug Men's Apparel Guild (MAGIC) convention (again)

Early Nov Specialty Equipment Manufacturers Association (SEMA) convention

Chronology

1598 > Spain claims what's now southern Nevada as part of the colony of New Mexico.

1829 > Mexican explorers name an unexpected oasis of grasslands "Las Vegas" – "The Meadows".

1847 > USA acquires New Mexico.

1855 > Mormons establish the colony of Bringhurst in the Las Vegas Valley; it lasts three years.

1864 > Nevada becomes a state.

1905 > The railroad arrives. Las Vegas is established on May 15, when forty newly drawn blocks are auctioned.

1909 > Nevada became the first US state to outlaw gambling.

1931 > Nevada marks the end of Prohibition by legalizing gambling – the only state to do so.

1935 > Hoover Dam completed. Las Vegas hosts first convention.

1938 > Guy McAfee, former chief of LA's vice squad, takes over the Pair-O-Dice Club, on what he dubs "The Strip".

1940 > Las Vegas's population reaches eight thousand.

1941 > El Rancho opens as the Strip's first fully fledged resort.

1946 > Mobster "Bugsy" Siegel opens the Flamingo; he's murdered six months later after heavy losses.

1950s > An unstoppable flow of new Strip resorts includes the Desert Inn, the Sands, the Riviera, the Dunes and the Hacienda. Desert A-bomb tests can be seen and heard from the city.

1966 > Caesars Palace, the first themed casino, opens. Howard Hughes asked to leave the Desert Inn because he isn't gambling; instead, he buys it, along with the Sands, the Silver Slipper and the New Frontier, marking the end of Mob domination.

1969 > Kirk Kerkorian opens the world's largest hotel– the Las Vegas Hilton – which hosts Elvis's rebirth as a karate-kicking lounge lizard.

1973 > Kirk Kerkorian again opens the world's largest hotel – the original MGM Grand, now Bally's. Steve Wynn takes over downtown's Golden Nugget.

1983 > Following disastrous fires at the MGM Grand and the Hilton, Las Vegas seems about to be eclipsed by Atlantic City; direct flights between New York and Las Vegas are discontinued.

1989 > Steve Wynn opens the opulent Mirage, complete with volcano. Benny Binion dies, with his Horseshoe downtown still Las Vegas's most profitable casino.

1993 > In a short-lived bid to reinvent Las Vegas as a child-friendly destination, Luxor, Treasure Island and the new MGM Grand all open.

1995 > Downtown roofed over to create Fremont Street Experience.

1997 > New York–New York opens; in a craze for building replica cities, it's followed by Bellagio in 1998 and the Venetian and Paris in 1999.

2000 > Steve Wynn sells the Mirage organization to MGM, which then buys the Mandalay Bay Group in 2004.

2005 > Harrah's buys Caesars Entertainment, leaving the Strip largely owned by two huge corporations. Steve Wynn opens Wynn Las Vegas.

2009 > Recession hits hard. MGM Mirage completes CityCenter, but many projects are abandoned.

2011 > Former mob lawyer Oscar Goodman completes a twelve-year stint as mayor, succeeded by wife Carolyn.

2014 > The Las Vegas High Roller and SLS open for action on the Strip.

PUBLISHING INFORMATION

This second edition published September 2015 by **Rough Guides Ltd**

80 Strand, London WC2R 0RL

11, Community Centre, Panchsheel Park, New Delhi 110017, India

Distributed by Penguin Random House

Penguin Books Ltd, 80 Strand, London WC2R 0RL

Penguin Group (USA) 345 Hudson Street, NY 10014, USA

Penguin Group (Australia) 250 Camberwell Road, Camberwell, Victoria 3124, Australia

Penguin Group (NZ) 67 Apollo Drive, Mairangi Bay, Auckland 1310, New Zealand

Penguin Group (South Africa) Block D, Rosebank Office Park, 181 Jan Smuts Avenue,
Parktown North, Gauteng, South Africa 2193

Rough Guides is represented in Canada by

Tourmaline Editions Inc., 662 King Street West, Suite 304, Toronto, Ontario, M5V 1M7

Typeset in Minion and Din to an original design by Henry Iles and Dan May.

Printed and bound in China

© Rough Guides, 2015

Maps © Rough Guides

144pp includes index

A catalogue record for this book is available from the British Library

ISBN 978-0-24118 684-8

The publishers and authors have done their best to ensure the accuracy and currency of all the
information in **Pocket Rough Guide Las Vegas**, however, they can accept no responsibility for
any loss, injury, or inconvenience sustained by any traveller as a result of information or advice
contained in the guide.

1 3 5 7 9 8 6 4 2

ROUGH GUIDES CREDITS

Editors: Rebecca Hallett, Alison Roberts
Layout: Pradeep Thapliyal, Umesh Aggarwal
Cartography: Edward Wright
Picture editors: Aude Vauconsant, Mark Thomas
Photographer: Tim Draper
Proofreaders: Anita Sach, Susannah Wight
Managing editors: Andy Turner,
Mani Ramaswamy

Production: Nicole Landau, Charlotte Cade
Cover design: Nicole Newman
Editorial Assistant: Freya Godfrey
Senior pre-press designer: Dan May
Publisher: Joanna Kirby
Publishing director: Georgina Dee

THE AUTHOR

Greg Ward has been writing about Las Vegas for more than twenty years. As well as four previous
Rough Guides to the city, he's the author of separate Rough Guides to the Southwest USA and the
Grand Canyon. He has also written many other Rough Guides, including those to the USA, the *Titanic*,
Hawaii, Brittany & Normandy, Provence, Spain, Blues CDs and US History; edited many more; and
written books for several other publishers. For more information, visit Ⓦ www.gregward.info.

ACKNOWLEDGEMENTS

Greg Ward: Thanks as ever to my dear wife Sam, for her support, encouragement and wise words. At Rough Guides, thanks to Becca Hallett for her thoughtful and scrupulous editing, and Ed Wright for his exceptional dedication to producing great maps. And thanks to everyone in Las Vegas who helped me to find and enjoy the very best of the city, especially Kimberley Diller and David Gonzalez, as well as Hannah Allen, Jennifer Byles, Stephanie Capellas, Stephanie Chavez, Katie Conway, Maggie Feldman, Sara Gorgon, Andrew Ho, Alison Monaghan, Holly Olp, Jennifer Polito, Kellyann Roberts, Rochelle Samilin-Jurani, Josie Self, Melanie Shafer, Wendy Sloan, Eleni Stylianou, Melissa Warren and Cathy Wiedemer.

HELP US UPDATE

We've gone to a lot of effort to ensure that the second edition of the **Pocket Rough Guide Las Vegas** is accurate and up-to-date. However, things change – places get "discovered", opening hours are notoriously fickle, restaurants and rooms raise prices or lower standards. If you feel we've got it wrong or left something out, we'd like to know, and if you can remember the address, the price, the hours, the phone number, so much the better.

Please send your comments with the subject line "**Pocket Rough Guide Las Vegas Update**" to ✉mail@roughguides.com. We'll credit all contributions and send a copy of the next edition (or any other Rough Guide if you prefer) for the very best emails.

Find more travel information, connect with fellow travellers and book your trip on Ⓦwww .roughguides.com

PHOTO CREDITS

All images © Rough Guides except the following:

Front cover Hard Rock Hotel sign © Stock Connection/SuperStock
Cover flap Red Rock Canyon © Corbis/Tim Fitzharris (tr); The Little White Chapel © Corbis/Fraser Hall (cl)
Back cover The Bellagio Fountains © AWL Images/Mark Sykes
p.1 The Strip © AWL Images/Gavin Hellier
p.2 The Forum, Caesars Palace © Corbis/Maisant Ludovic
p.4 The Eiffel Tower, Paris© AWL Images/Alan Copson
p.5 View from Paris's Eiffel Tower © Getty Images/Mark A Johnson
p.6 New York–New York © Getty Images/Robert Harding
p.8 The Forum Shops © Ed Wright (c)
p.11 The monorail © Corbis/Jon Hicks (b)
p.15 Bellagio © Getty Images/Robert Harding (t); Hoover Dam © Corbis/Kerrick James (cr)
p.16 Kà ©Eric Jamison
p.17 Terry Fator © Tomek Pleskaczynski Photography (t); Jubilee! © Denise Truscello (b)
p.19 Mon Ami Gabi © Alamy/Hemis (tl)
p.25 Las Vegas High Roller © Corbis/Gene Blevins (b)
p.26 Zion National Park © Getty Images/Jordan Siemens
p.27 Valley of Fire © Corbis Bridge (tl); Grand Canyon South Rim © Alamy/Russ Bishop (tr);

Red Rock Canyon © Realy Easy Star (c); Grand Canyon West Rim © Julie Quarry (b)
pp.28–29 Neon lights, downtown © AWL Images/Walter Bibikow
p.31 Jellyfish, Shark Reef © Alamy/Gail Mooney-Kelly
p.51 Jean Philippe Patisserie © Corbis/Barry Sweet
p.66 Jersey Boys © Joan Marcus
p.67 Jubilee! © Denise Truscello
p.69 The Volcano, The Mirage © Corbis/Richard Cummins
p.85 Terry Fator © Getty Images/Ethan Miller
p.98 Sam's Town 300 NASCAR race © Corbis/Warren Wimmer/Icon SMI
p.99 Sunset Station at night © Sunset Station
p.104 Red Rock Canyon © Getty Images/John P Kelly
p.106 Hoover Dam © Corbis/Kerrick James
p.107 Valley of Fire State Park © Getty Images/Tom Till
p.109 Skywalk, Grand Canyon West © National Geographic Image Collection (t); Hopi Point, Grand Canyon South Rim © Alamy/Tom Bean (b)
p.110 Zion Narrows, Zion National Park © Getty Images/David Epperson
pp.112–113 Pool, Caesars Palace © Corbis/Topic Photo Agency
pp.122–123 Sign © SuperStock/Ron Chapple Photography

Index

Maps are marked in **bold**.

SO NOW WE'VE TOLD YOU ABOUT THE THINGS NOT TO MISS, THE BEST PLACES TO STAY, THE TOP RESTAURANTS, THE LIVELIEST BARS AND THE MOST SPECTACULAR SIGHTS, IT ONLY SEEMS FAIR TO TELL YOU ABOUT THE BEST TRAVEL INSURANCE AROUND